a search for common ground

BROADMAN PRESS
Nashville, Tennessee

© Copyright 1977 • Broadman Press.

All rights reserved.

4265–33

ISBN: 0–8054–6533–2

Dewey Decimal Classification: 289.9

Subject Headings: NEO—PENTECOSTALISM//
　　　　　　　　　　CHARISMATIC MOVEMENT

Library of Congress Catalog Card Number: 77-79608

Printed in the United States of America

Contents

Introduction: The New-New Pentecostals		5
1.	The Spirit in Romanesque	20
2.	The Spirit in Search of a Biblical Theology	29
3.	Tongues of Change	49
4.	What to Do?	65
	Conclusion: The Late 1970s Amid Winds	83
	Bibliography	92

Unless otherwise noted, all Scripture quotations are taken from the King James Version of the Bible.

Scripture quotations marked RSV are taken from the Revised Standard Version.

Scripture quotations marked Phillips are taken from *The New Testament in Modern English,* © J. B. Phillips, 1958, 1960, 1972.

Introduction: The New-New Pentecostals

Eutychus V, the patron saint of holy humor in *Christianity Today,* tells of an embarrassing moment for him:

> The other night my children were yukking it up about the night of Dad's hand under the bed . . . .
> It all began when one of my seminary professors asked my wife and me to occupy his house during his vacation . . . . The house was situated so that the lights of every car coming down the road flashed into the master bedroom. I usually find it hard to sleep in a strange place, and my difficulty was increased by the continual flashing of auto headlights.
> Finally, I put my arm over my eyes to block out the lights and dropped into an uneasy sleep. Unknowingly, I also cut off the circulation in that arm.
> In the wee hours of the morning, some sound woke me. I sat up, causing my now feelingless arm to dangle over the edge of the bed. As I groggily reached for my glasses, I encountered my own cold and clammy hand.
> With a shudder of horror, I jumped to a standing position in the middle of the bed and shouted, "There's a hand under the bed!"
> At that, my wife bolted out of bed and began groping along the wall for the light switch. I joined her in the frantic search.
> Suddenly a thought came to me: "Why am I using only one hand?" Even before I found the light switch, the awful truth had dawned on me, and I knew of the years of total recall my wife would have of that night.[1]

Eutychus V may spin a good yarn, but he knows little of

applying the "morals" of his own stories. Obviously, the "Case of the Clammy Hand" has implications for the present encounter between traditional Christians and a people collectively known as neo-Pentecostals. The two groups may disagree as to which is the "clammy" one, but members of each group know within the depths of their being that they are part of the same body. Coexistence is not only desirable but also mandatory for balance in the Christian experience. This feeling is becoming increasingly prevalent in the light of the growing number of persons who identify with Bishop Pike's description of himself as one of the "alumni of the church."

The alternative to understanding is a growing number of split churches and neo-Pentecostals living in fear and pity for the non-Pentecostal. The phenomenon of joyless, automatic Christian lives, robbed of the power of the Holy Spirit, will continue unless understanding and sharing from both sides receives high priority on the local level.

This book is designed to increase understanding on the part of both sides of the non/neo sides of Pentecostalism. Little is to be gained by either side's hurling insults at the other. When the current charismatic fever pitch has cooled, isolation on either side will be costly to both sides of an emotional but fruitful issue.

Why Rapid Growth?

The 1970s find Pentecostals in at least twenty-one organized denominations led in size by the Assembly of God churches, who have more than a million members in nine thousand local churches. Even more remarkable are the growing numbers of Pentecostals not aligned with traditional Pentecostal groups. Another three million charis-

INTRODUCTION: THE NEW-NEW PENTECOSTALS

matics fit into this category. These persons are more likely than not to attend Sunday-morning worship at a Catholic or mainline Protestant church.

Black Roots

The fact that the number of these neo-Pentecostals has grown at a phenomenal rate is due to a number of factors. Often overlooked are the black origins of the current Pentecostal wave. There are currently at least 800,000 members of fourteen all-black Pentecostal denominations and perhaps an equal number in the storefront churches of the ghetto with names like "Mother Jackson's Spirit-filled House of Prayer and Healing."

The black roots of white Pentecostalism can be easily traced back to 1906 in Los Angeles, where a small group of black believers met on Azusa Street in Los Angeles. A black minister named W. J. Seymour had migrated there from Houston. He gathered a group of black-skinned saints into homes to pray for a recurrence of apostolic signs and miracles. The prayers were answered, and the signs included tongues-speaking. News of the outpouring quickly spread across the nation.

C. H. Mason, the overseer of the Church of God in Christ, went to the Azusa Street site to investigate. He came back to Memphis speaking in tongues. This movement is today the largest black Pentecostal group in America.

Segregated Pentecostalism still predominates in America in spite of some attempts to celebrate the Spirit across color lines. One such attempt is the International Church of the Four-Square Gospel, which still has headquarters in Azusa. As long as such minimal attempts at integration remain the pattern, the black roots of modern Pentecostalism will remain undiscovered and unappreciated by most.

New Daring

The Holy Spirit spreads freedom—that is his task. The renewed courage to worship creatively on the part of some Christian leaders is due to a brief glimpse of how they can know freedom in spite of structure. These people engaged in the process of becoming free are inspiring others to know freedom in spite of structures. They are helping others know the freedom of the Spirit in spite of culturally dictated roles.

One such outstanding denominational leader in a leading traditional convention office sat down one afternoon and wrote the following meditation, showing the new daring that is his.

> Just before this denomination died . . . and came to life again . . . .
>
> They talked about being creative and innovative; but just as sure as someone thought of a way for a church to be creative and innovative that did not include all the archaic organization, he got "the ecclesiastical quelch."
>
> They insisted there was no money for new and creative programs while hundreds of denominational "problem solvers" as cold as the computers they relied upon dashed madly about the nation, seemingly intent on burning up the world's supply of jet fuel.
>
> They met in their annual conventions, living in the best hotels, eating the best meals, using the most sophisticated multimedia—but they did not cause a ripple in the headlines. Meanwhile, a sect with only 10 percent of their membership present came to town and attracted twice as many people. They stayed in the homes of people and sought to evangelize

INTRODUCTION: THE NEW-NEW PENTECOSTALS

> them. They cooked their meals out of doors in huge kettles and made the headlines every day. All the *ecclesiastical* junior executives wondered why.
>
> The young, bright-eyed, open people were saying, "No hard-nosed, open, charismatic man can come to a place of leadership in our denomination."
>
> Churches still inspired by the missionary and evangelistic vision continued to give money to support growing institutions that became less and less missionary and evangelistic.
>
> They became more and more captured by their middle-class culture, afraid to face the demands of the third world and the counter culture. Increasingly they became less and less aware of the growing pain of the dispossessed, the disinherited, and the disappointed of the world . . . and the denomination died for lack of *spirit*.

This plaintive cry came from a denominational leader yearning for the people he loves around him to know freedom. He is part of a new breed of mildly charismatic leaders who are pumping new life into old forms.

Direct Experience

One reason that there are in 1977 more than four million active Pentecostals is that believers are discovering that Christian discipleship can be more than dry ritual. Pentecostal churches are overflowing partially because one finds there a direct, personal experience of God's reality. Shouts, handclapping, impromptu singing, and marching in the aisles are testimonies to the outside world that God is warm and real and present.

Modern technology, like man's electronic extension in television, has brought man of age and threatens to rob him of his need for mystery. But just when some were saying man could get along as though God does not exist, others were plunging into the explosion of the charismatic.

Sociologist Bagdikiam credits much of this situation to information overload. He says:

> It's not too much to suggest that we may already have reached an intolerable limit for many persons. Many people today reject rationality and sequential systematic thought, and turn instead to the instinctive and subjective life. They have been abstracted beyond human meaning. There is a limit to how much you can withdraw the human personality from direct, emotional experience. So all the beautiful methods of inundating the society with abstract information could provide a starvation of emotion.[2]

This overload has caused man to become experience oriented and has helped give rise to charismatic renewal.

People-centered

Mainline Pentecostals do not major on fancy buildings with accompanying debts and mortgages. This lack of "edifice complex" has allowed Pentecostals to stay on the job in inner-city slums in urban America. This desperately needy mission field is one from which many "respectable" Protestants have fled for racial or economic reasons while they listened to sermons on equality and ministry.

Fortunately, this trend, which seems to picture the Protestant pastor as a frustrated real estate agent wanting to build monuments, has not affected the neo-Pentecostals either. Even upper-class, suburban charismatics have not concentrated on buildings but people. White socks mix with white Cadillacs in buildings not impressive for their size as much as their warmth and freedom. The individual can feel at home immediately.

Mysticism

There is an increasing and sustained interest in tran-

INTRODUCTION: THE NEW-NEW PENTECOSTALS

scendental experience, including mysticism, which has come from Eastern religions. Zen has laid the foundation in the current generation of youth. It first taught them such phrases as "Whatever turns you on" and "Do your own thing." Next Zen used the *koan* or answerless riddle to expand the logical way of viewing life.

This search for the supernatural has ended up in such avenues as the occult, with its emphasis on nonlogical ways of knowing. Transcendental Meditation promises inner bliss and healing through two twenty-minute sessions of meditation every day. This mystical approach feeds fire to the idea that there is much to be learned outside the strict use of the intellect.

Powerful Personalities

There is already a large collection of "folk heroes" among the new Pentecostals. These well-known and powerful personalities are helping to popularize the Spirit-related experiences among a vast segment of new believers. Among these persons is Pat Boone, the darling of the graying bobby-soxer set. Mr. Boone and his family are well known in the entertainment world.

In the late 1960s, Pat Boone was kicked out of his local Church of Christ in Los Angeles for speaking in tongues. He later repented and was reinstated by the elders into full fellowship with congregation. In the 1970s, however, Mr. Boone was disfellowshipped again—this time for baptizing new converts in his own swimming pool and for his emphasis on faith healing. Nonetheless, Pat and Shirley Boone continue to spread the news of the advantages of the Spirit-filled life.

David Wilkerson of *The Cross and the Switchblade* fame

continues to travel and write about the flame of the Spirit within him. He is capturing the imagination of many youthful Christians, including in his message a stress on the imminent return of Christ.

Oral Roberts, complete with a vast educational and mass-media empire in Tulsa at Oral Roberts University, is busy cranking out a combination of Pentecostalism and New Thought. His "seed faith" and "prayer language" messages are indicative of this blend of theology. Affluent Americans, hitherto untouched by the old-line Pentecostalism (or, for that matter, the "old" Oral Roberts approach before he joined the United Methodist Church) are being reached by Reverend Roberts' blend of big business and spiritual concerns.

During the presidential campaign of 1976, there came to light one Jean Carter Stapleton, the sister of candidate Jimmy Carter. She writes books and articles and gives lectures on the power of the Spirit in psychological healing. Many thousands of Americans were introduced to Mrs. Stapleton as representative of one type of Spirit-filled ministry.

Small Groups

The small-group movement within evangelicalism and such other groupings as Catholicism has led to wide involvement in the neo-Pentecostal movement. Such persons as Keith Miller and such movements as "renewal" and "cursillio" have fed the fire of spiritual filling. Persons involved in small groups are saying much the same things to traditional churches as are the neo-Pentecostals. (Indeed, at times these persons are one and the same.)

The messages to the churches include:

INTRODUCTION: THE NEW-NEW PENTECOSTALS

1. *"I want to touch."* You will probably not see me in your church services next Sunday if you expect me to sit in an auditorium in a pew lined up neatly with the others. Looking at the back of someone's head does not lend itself to creating Christian fellowship. In the Bible we are told to "greet one another with a holy kiss." The spiritual truth behind that is that physical comforting is a part of fellowship. Services seem cold without physical contact.

2. *"Don't program me."* The Spirit blows where he will. Attempts to program him into such activities as the same worship format Sunday after Sunday *or* the annual spring revival kill the spontaneity of the Spirit. Worship should flow with the warmth of the Spirit's presence.

3. *"I want to celebrate."* I want a church in which I am free to praise the Lord in openness. Occasionally I may even want to raise my hands heavenward and say "Amen" or "Praise the Lord." Services that are not positive and built on praise will not attract me on a regular basis.

The Collective Unconscious

Psychologist Carl Jung maintained that each human being is heir to a wave of ideas and impressions from previous generations within our general culture. This he called "collective unconscious."

There are movements within Christendom that have suppressed emphasis on the Holy Spirit for generations. This collective depriving has built up over the years an intense hunger for things of the Spirit. This hunger is now bursting forth in the more formal churches in the form of the neo-Pentecostal movement.

Movement Away from Churches

Each year in the 1970s there has been an ever-so-slight

indication of a decrease in church participation on the part of Americans. It is difficult to say which is cause and which is effect, but disconsolate persons are finding solace in Pentecostal groups instead of in more formal church expressions. The search for identity in a mobile society lends itself more to the immediate acceptance of a small-group experience. The anxiety of nonacceptance is solved by participation with Spirit-filled persons.

Superstition

In times of crises, political or economic, human beings tend to revert to superstition. In effect, therein lies one's faith system. For example, Martin Luther wrote a volume in which he denied that demons could cause illness. He was operating on an intellectual plane. When his friend Phillip Melanchthon became ill, Mr. Luther immediately commanded the demons to leave him.

When a president resigns during the heat of controversy—especially when his people's most widespread faith is in a form of civil religion that allows them to salute the Christian and American flags at the same moment—panic sets in. The people turn to new, less established ways of knowing and being. Among those ways is the new Pentecostalism.

A rabbi has described the 1970s in terms of political involvement as "lobotomized passivity." It is as if an operation has been performed on the consciences of Americans. The civil rights movements, for example, have quietened down. This relaxation allows the pendulum between the pietist and activist to swing back toward the spiritual. The pendulum may stop in the middle in the 1980s when the intense heat of the new wave of Pentecos-

INTRODUCTION: THE NEW-NEW PENTECOSTALS

talism is over. In the meantime, the politically disoriented are drawn to new forms of religious expression.

Powerful Parachurch Organizations

The fires of new Pentecostalism are being fanned by organizations that operate outside traditional church expression. One such organization is the Full Gospel Businessmen's Fellowship, International. With a large publishing and mass-media empire, this group has made Pentecostalism palatable to some who would otherwise remain ignorant of the movement. City-wide meetings revolving around a meal attract dozens to try speaking in tongues. Logos International serves as a publishing arm along with Charisma Books, and together they reach hundreds of thousands of readers. This is but one of the parachurch movements pushing the Pentecostal movement along.

The FGBMFI publishes a multicolored monthly magazine entitled *Voice,* featuring testimonies of those who have been baptized by the Spirit (Box 17904, Los Angeles, CA. 90017).

Loss of Confidence in Science

In the 1960s, theologians wrote books like *The Secular City* by Harvey Cox. In this work, the author calls upon his reader to celebrate man's achievements in the building of metropolises. According to this book, in this postreligious age there is really no need for God anymore.

Science was being hailed as the savior of mankind when the 1970s dawned. Man was promised that cancer, war, racism, hatred, and poverty would vanish in the face of the unstoppable onslaught of scientific research.

The mid-1970s saw that trend reversed. Science could no longer be hailed as general deliverer to all of man's problems. As a result, many scientists have become spiritual in orientation. The pendulum swings.

Response to this remarkable happening called *new Pentecostalism* has been varied. New rules are needed for this new happening. It is no longer fair or accurate to react to Pentecostalism as if it were confined to a small group of Pentecostal denominations located "across the track" and characterized by rolling in the aisles. This is partly due to the fact that the new Pentecostals have certain characteristics that are not the same as those shared by the old-line established Pentecostals—such groups as the Assemblies of God. These characteristics include the facts that the new Pentecostals are:

1. Lay-centered.—The new Pentecostalism centers around nonordained persons who generally function as Bible teachers within small groups. Yet, there is a commendable absence of anticlericalism. A more personal and informal form of ministry is replacing the stiff, formal style some associate with the old forms of clergy functions.

2. Composed of varied liturgy.—The new Pentecostal participant is likely to be a part of a group that varies its worship patterns. Worship may be structured or unstructured. In worship, labels of *liberal* or *conservative* do not fit. Renewal is promoted without being tied to any particular program of reform.

3. Concerned with the dignity of the person.—The new Pentecostal is a part of the worldwide movement toward liberation. The Spirit is freeing persons from bonds of inhibition, fear, or self-pity. Hunger for personal experience is leading to a positive, interpersonal, *called* freedom

INTRODUCTION: THE NEW-NEW PENTECOSTALS

in the Spirit. This growth is happening outside the church walls of old-time Pentecostalism. A life-style of dignity is imparted. A renewal is happening because individuals are confessing, experiencing, and finding acceptance.

Intelligent and responsible reaction to the new Pentecostalism is partly dependent on the knowledge of the economic, political, social, and historical factors leading to its growth. Events of the religious realm do not happen in isolation. There are always a number of factors leading to periodic renewals of the Spirit.

These statements are proven true by the history of the church. What is going on in the late 1970s is not new, except for this generation. Church history records many ebbs and flows in terms of the power of the Spirit.

The church began (some say at Pentecost) with emphasis on the Spirit. Paul gave the Holy Spirit proper emphasis and counseled balance in the awareness of the Spirit's presence. This was followed by a long period of deemphasis of the Spirit in Western Christianity. Even reformers like Calvin and Luther succeeded in imprisoning the Spirit within the text of Scripture, the Word of God. Baptists and others in the Radical Reformation, which moved further away from Catholicism than did Luther, stressed the importance of the Spirit; gradually, however, the Holy Spirit was captivated into a conventionality as the centuries passed. The reappearance of the Spirit today is a partial remedy to that tragedy.

Given historical perspective, it is remarkable that some Baptists today are behaving as the "establishment" toward the new Pentecostals. This is a new and uncomfortable position for sons of the Radical Reformation. Lacking historical or social perspective, some have overreacted out of confusion.

For example, one state convention in an annual meeting voted against a study committee to ascertain "biblical teaching on the charismatic movement." The motion presenter closed with the observation that "there is a great movement of the Holy Spirit in the churches. We ought to be in the forefront of what is happening." [3] The convention voted not to do the study.

Other responses have been more open and positive. They have been largely the result of a patient understanding of the reasons for growth of the new Pentecostalism, a knowledge of some specific instances of it, biblical knowledge of the Spirit's role, wisdom concerning the use of tongues, and practical but gentle steps in response to the presence of some Spirit-filled persons.

The chapters that follow in this book are designed to provide such information and suggestions for a positive response to the new Pentecostals.

Chapter 1 discusses the impact of the new Pentecostalism on the Roman Catholic church as a type. What is happening there is happening in other forms of Christianity, with some differences.

Chapter 2 is a discussion of the biblical basis of a Holy Spirit study. Key passages are interpreted without avoiding controversial ones.

The thorny issue of speaking in tongues is the subject of chapter 3. This divisive topic is examined from biblical and other helpful viewpoints.

Chapter 4 is a seminar on how a local church might respond to the presence of new Pentecostalism in its community and fellowship. Practical helps are given.

The book concludes with a plea for peaceful coexistence

in the warmth-giving life of the Spirit.

Being on mission in God's world is responding to the call to make disciples of all persons. "All persons" includes those who are unlike us, even to the degree of variant forms of Christianity. As surely as Jesus wills us to be his disciples, we should respond to the presence of others with love. This book can help. The author prays so.

NOTES

1. "Eutychus and His Kin," *Christianity Today* (16 February 1973), p. 37.
2. Quoted by Walker Knight and Everett Hullum, "Hello, Hello, Is Anybody Out There?" *Home Missions* (January 1974), p. 19.
3. From *The Christian Index* (21 November 1974), p. 1.

1. The Spirit in Romanesque

Vatican Council II was a major force in opening up the Roman Catholic Church to a renewed emphasis on the Holy Spirit. Pope John XXIII opened the conference of the mid-1960s with a promise to open a window and let in a breath of fresh air. As is the case often when the Spirit comes, it was fresh air all right—accompanied by a mighty wind.

The spirit of renewal and reformation within the Catholic Church was let loose. Two laymen on the faculty at Duquesne University were stimulated in the spring of 1966 when they realized that their discipleship did not have the power that they noted was present in the New Testament. They prayed often and let their concern be known to the other faculty members.

In late summer of that same year, two young men attending the National Cursillio Convention (a renewal movement born in the Catholic Church in Europe in the late 1940s and stressing the need for a personal relationship with Jesus) introduced into their small group David Wilkerson's *The Cross and the Switchblade*. Early the next year, contact was initiated with some non-Catholic Pentecostals in Pittsburgh. A few weeks later several Duquesne faculty members were "baptized in the Spirit."

News of the Pittsburgh happening reached the University of Notre Dame almost as soon as the incident occurred. Home prayer meetings were started with the aid of the Full Gospel Businessmen's Fellowship. The number of persons receiving the Holy Spirit mushroomed in the Catholic community at Notre Dame.

Shortly after Easter in 1967, the first annual "National Catholic Pentecostal Conference" was held with about one hundred students in attendance. That conference continues to grow; more than thirty-five thousand were in attendance in 1976. The conference has also become international in scope.

Also at Notre Dame, a communications center was established in 1969. It was specifically to serve as an information and inspiration network to the Catholic Pentecostal movement. Published at the center is a directory of Catholic charismatic prayer groups. The current issue (June 1976) lists more than twenty-six hundred groups in the United States.

An attractive thirty-six-page monthly magazine entitled *New Covenant* is now published and has an increasing circulation. Each issue centers around a specific theme. These themes include healing (November 1973), about which it is said that there are four major types of healing that God is seeking to bring to the whole man. They are:

1. Evangelistic healing—which includes the proclamation of the gospel toward spiritual healing.

2. Commitment healing—which includes a commitment to our Lord.

3. Radical healing—which includes not being bound to get angry, irritated, or frustrated.

4. Growth healing—which includes ongoing healing in human life, resulting from free interaction in a caring community.[1]

The February 1974 issue of *New Covenant* focuses on "The Christian and World Events." In speaking of the most common criticism of Pentecostalism, that it is not socially relevant, the author of the feature article contends that contemplation, if put first, will lead to political awareness and action.[2]

The October 1974 issue of *New Covenant* stresses evangelism. Father Bill O'Brien, a priest, writes: "The renewal of the ministry of evangelism means renewing our enthusiasm for spreading the Good News . . . . May each of us catch the fire and enthusiasm of the Holy Spirit for proclaiming the Word." [3]

The November 1974 issue revolves around the theme of community.[4] Claiming that the recent charismatic renewal communities hold the promise of renewal for all of Christian life, the author points out five characteristics of such renewal-inspiring groups:

1. They do not ignore the demands of normal human existence.
2. They do not flee the material order.
3. They find power in worship and prayer.
4. They act upon the social demands of the gospel.
5. They develop a community finding its main expression in love.

As one can see immediately, *New Covenant* continues to serve as a prophetic voice for what is now a well-organized Catholic charismatic movement. In 1977, about one million American Catholics (out of a total of forty-nine million) are deeply involved in the charismatic movement. Such a large movement cannot be ignored by sensitive, but more traditional, Catholic and Protestant Christians.

THE SPIRIT IN ROMANESQUE

One example of this statement is the fact that in 1969, the American Catholic bishops decided to allow the charismatic renewal within the Catholic Church to have free rein. The official report contains these elements:

1. Prudent priests should be assigned to be involved in the movement.
2. Judgment of the validity of the claims of the movement should be made by observing the effects on those who participate in the prayer meetings.
3. The movement has a legitimate and strong biblical base.
4. Judgments should not be based on superficial knowledge.
5. The movement should be dissociated from "classic" Pentecostalism.

The report was, however, a bit premature in its judgment that "this phenomenon is not a movement in the full sense of the word. It has no national structure."

This report was reinforced by a similar one in 1972, which stated that the movement was to be commended for its emphasis on prayer, ongoing conversion, and devotion to the church and sacraments.

Not all Catholics have been so kind toward the movement. In the December 1973 issue of *U.S. Catholic*, Frank O'Meara says that Catholic Pentecostalism is a sign of something wrong in the church, but "it is not the cure." [5] He criticizes the new charismatics for their naive use of the Bible, artificial inducement to speaking in tongues, possible self-delusion that comes with openness to the gifts of the Spirit, and forcing the Holy Spirit into the service of men.

In a significant reader's poll in the same issue, 53 percent of the respondents said that the movement is dangerous because it draws away from social service; 53 percent said tongues and healing distract from the main mission of the church; and 60 percent said it short-cuts the normal process of Christian growth in grace. Ironically, 63 percent said that they thought the movement will do more good than harm for the church.

This reflection of mixed feelings among Catholics regarding the Pentecostal movement within their ranks is almost universal. These feelings are true also of Catholic reaction to the current reformation going on in the church. Movement toward the Holy Spirit is only one of the symptoms indicating that what has gone on inside the Catholic Church over the past decade is indeed a reformation. Other symptoms include a renewal of interest in Bible study. Evangelism, as indicated above, is now central to many Catholics affected by the recent reformation.

New worship forms are also indicative of the reformation. Pentecostalism is serving as one stimulus to new worship forms. In fact, Brother David S. K. Stindl-Rast says that the current charismatic renewal is first and last a renewal of worship. He warns against a new ritual form already emerging in the well-organized Catholic Pentecostal movement. The force of renewal cannot be formalized, he argues. Even the Spirit-filled one in a worship setting must rely on the manifestation of his Spirit, not the display of our gifts.[6]

New worship forms initiated by the current Pentecostal movement are forming. This change of forms threatens established Catholic practices; but the threat can be an impetus to renewal, provided neither side becomes too rigid. This is particularly true because of the increasingly responsible roles that Catholic lay persons are filling today. Those without formal theological training bring a spontaneity to Christian experience that must be balanced by the wisdom of biblical knowledge. The result can continue to be the beautiful, but disturbing, experience of reformation.

Hopefully, the movement of the Spirit will continue toward continued dialogue between Protestants and Catholics, Pentecostals and non-Pentecostals. The Spirit may even transcend the barriers of such labels as liberal and conservative. One day believers may be known as simply as they were in Antioch—that is, as Christ–ians. This possibility exists because the Spirit is free to promote renewal in the church without being bound to any specific program of reform.

An imaginary visit to a small-group prayer meeting involving participants in the Catholic Pentecostal movement is revealing. This is the typical form of meeting for the movement, after all, and carries within itself its own strengths and weaknesses. It is the central public action of the movement. Composed chiefly of lay people, the meetings are spontaneous and have no officially designated leader. One usually emerges, however, as does a worship format, over a period of weeks. This occurrence keeps the meetings from being what an outsider could call chaotic. Frequent periods of silent contemplation are mixed with group singing, accompanied by a guitar, group praising and praying, testimonies, reading of the Bible, coffee breaks and informal fellowship, and prayer for and with those who wish "to receive the Holy Spirit." Occasional singing, praying, and praising are done in tongues or "prayer languages." Non-Pentecostals often leave such meetings impressed with the inoffensive manner in which the gifts of the Spirit are manifested. They may be impressed further by the joy, love, and praise into which they feel drawn.

Despite criticism, Catholic participation in Pentecostalism has usually led the Catholics to a deeper appreciation for the church and its sacraments. Penance, confession, and the mass are not abandoned but given deeper meaning by the Spirit. These may be occasionally redefined by the Catholic charismatic, but even then are held in deep reverence.

Evangelicals have been greatly pleased by one development in the current charismatic interest. It seems that interest in the third person of the Trinity has resulted in attention to the second—Jesus the Christ. Baptism in the Spirit is viewed by most in the movement as an outgrowth of a deepening personal relationship with Jesus Christ. Indeed, one official observer of the movement states, "Without this act of faith, our practice of Catholicism may be a religion, but it is neither Catholicism or Christianity." [7]

His report, containing the imprimatur of the Bishop of Fort Wayne-South Bend, contains a form of the "plan of salvation" with which evangelicals are intimately familiar. Mr. Byrne recommends:

1. Consider Jesus.
2. Consider your own state.
3. Turn to God . . .
4. Turn to Jesus . . . Ask him to be the Lord of your life . . .
5. Consider what happened . . .
6. Place yourself quietly in his presence.[8]

Conclusion

The continuing "watch and see" attitude of the National Conference of Catholic Bishops toward the Pentecostal movement within their ranks seems an appropriate one. Meanwhile, evangelical Protestants, whether charismatic or not, can celebrate the revival that the movement is fostering. It is the cohesive, constant nature of the Trinity that study of each of the persons within it tends to draw believers toward the other two. Despite human attempts to fragment or overemphasize one to the detriment of the other two, it is apparent that God in three persons is innately one.

So what began as an interest in the Spirit is resulting in a rediscovery of personal faith in the Son and the Father. *Hallelujah!* say the Protestants who have waited four hundred years for this to occur among their fellow Christians called Catholics.

Small prayer groups continue to be the core of the movement, as with all neo-Pentecostal groups. Within this fact lies the greatest possible danger of the movement. Uninformed, well-meaning but overzealous individuals can thwart the freeing power of the Spirit by becoming power-mad or bent on potentially dangerous practices such as completely supplanting medical practice. Within those same small groups lies also the potential for the discovery that there are other believers who also stumble and soar in their pilgrimage.

Catholic Pentecostalism is considered here as a type of what is going on among other Christian groups, particularly in the United States. Episcopal churches are also being affected. John L. Sherrill's work, *They Speak with Other Tongues*,[9] was an early account of the neo-

Pentecostal influence upon an Episcopal church and was written even before the movement had a name or attracted much attention. Methodists, Presbyterians, and Lutherans have been "hit," as have Baptists. Reaction has varied from swift labeling of the movement as "satanic," accompanied by official condemnation, to "wait and see" to open-armed acceptance.

The Spirit is about, even among the Catholics, to the pleasant surprise of almost everyone—including the folk called Christian.

NOTES

1. From *New Covenant* (November 1973), pp. 12 ff.
2. From *New Covenant* (February 1974), p. 13.
3. From *New Covenant* (October 1974), p. 11.
4. From *New Covenant* (November 1974), p. 14.
5. From *U.S. Catholic* (December 1973), p. 14.
6. David S. K. Stindl-Rast, "Charismatic Renewal," *Worship* 48, no. 7, pp. 382 ff.
7. James Byrne, *Threshold of God's Promise* (Notre Dame: Ave Maria Press, 1971), p. 49.
8. Ibid., p. 42.
9. John L. Sherrill, *They Speak with Other Tongues* (New York: Pyramid Books, 1964).

2. The Spirit in Search of a Biblical Theology

Reader, be warned!

It is the premise of this chapter that the Bible sheds a lot of light on itself. This is especially true because of the way it is misquoted by new Pentecostals. Frequently the quoter says, "This is what the Bible teaches" when he really means what one verse or half-verse appears to him to mean at the moment.

Pentecostalism, old or new, can stand some biblical light. This is especially true when strands within the biblical witness about the Holy Spirit are seen as a unit. This unity can eliminate a lot of false ideas and fragmenting practices in the same Spirit who came to make us one.

In fact, the Holy Spirit and the Bible are in constant interaction. When the Bible is opened in faith, the Spirit illuminates the written word. To the two-pronged sources of revelation for the evangelical—that is, Jesus as the living Word and the Bible as the written Word—can be added the Holy Spirit as the present Word. It is he who brings to life that same Bible which has so much to say about him, from start to finish.

In almost every era too little attention is paid to the doctrine of the Holy Spirit, and this neglect inevitably results in a distortion of Christian doctrine and a resultant suffering on the part of Christian life and work. This statement has been borne out in the 1970s with the presence of neo-Pentecostalism.

According to the Bible, when we speak of the Holy Spirit, we are not speaking of a nebulous power, a vague essence of a holy "ghost."

The phrase *Holy Spirit* is very well suited to describe the deity of the Spirit, for even in the Old Testament the word *holy* is used to describe God.

In the New Testament, the Holy Spirit is always regarded as God. He is presented in such a way that his Godhood does not hamper divine unity. In other words, the consistent pattern is the Spirit as the third person of the Trinity.

The Bible makes it clear that the Holy Spirit was not born on the day of Pentecost (Acts 2).

The first biblical passage relating to the Spirit is Genesis 1:2, where it is said that the Spirit of God moved over the waters. This means that the whole work of creation stands under the moving of the Spirit. The Holy Spirit participates in the work of creation. Throughout the Old Testament, the Spirit is described as the breath of living things.

The Holy Spirit is also active in human affairs. When he comes upon a prophet, he communicates messages from God. When an Old Testament personality prophesied, he did so because the Spirit of the Lord was upon him and communicated a message through him. (See Mic. 3:8; Zech. 7:12; 2 Sam. 23:2.)

This idea is carried over into the New Testament, where the unity of the Spirit with Christ is emphasized. It is by the Spirit as life-giver that God operates in the world. This insight puts the virgin birth of Christ into a new perspective. As Jesus Christ was conceived by the Spirit, so were

THE SPIRIT IN SEARCH OF A BIBLICAL THEOLOGY 31

his whole life and ministry. It is even said that he was taught by the Spirit and that he healed in the Spirit. So the ministry of Jesus of Nazareth was begun in the Spirit, given power by the Spirit, and continued in the Spirit after the ascension.

The conclusion to be drawn is that no believer can abstract Son from Spirit, Spirit from Son, or either from the Father. This is particularly important in relation to the claims of some new Pentecostals that the Spirit saves a person after he has been saved in Jesus the first time.

The Holy Spirit who appeared frequently and powerfully in the Old Testament shone fully in the Savior. In Jesus God focused the Spirit into one person and presence. As such, Jesus was *the* prophet of which the Old Testament prophets were types.

Near the end of his ministry, Jesus spoke many farewell messages. Some of those are gathered around the theme of the Paraclete, who universalizes the presence of Jesus. He goes beyond the limits of space and time that the historical Jesus had.

There are five references to the Paraclete in Jesus' farewell discourses: John 14:15–18,25–27; 15:26–27; 16:7–11,13–15. Jesus is presented earlier in John as the Paraclete, the one who represents us before the Father (John 14:6). Jesus insisted that he was the Paraclete of the disciples already and would send "another" helper. "I will come to you," Jesus said in effect in John 14:18. There could be no stronger identification between Jesus and the Spirit.

The basic meaning of the word *Paraclete* is "one called alongside to help." In a word, the Paraclete takes over the role of Jesus. The Holy Spirit is "another Jesus." He is sent to replace Jesus among the believers and to do for them what Jesus did on earth. So if the Spirit is truly to represent Jesus, he has to remain bound to the person of Jesus. Jesus is God's ultimate word to mankind. The function of the Spirit is not to give some new revelation of his own, but to bear witness to Jesus and to draw out the implications of God's ultimate revelation in Christ.

It was to amplify Jesus' ministry that the Spirit came in "a rushing mighty wind" in Acts 2. Acts 2:33 makes the connection between the Spirit and the church. Because Jesus the Christ is so closely bound to his people, so is the Spirit of Christ. Corporate life in the body of Christ, to which believers are called, is also life in the Spirit held in common. In Acts 2 the Holy Spirit comes as power, but he is the same Spirit who appeared to Micah, Samuel, and Jesus.

The Spirit comes also in movement. He is constantly described in the Bible with such word pictures as wind, air, and water. As Jesus posed verbs in answer to questions (come, see, love, suffer, become), so the Spirit is presented in motion. This is a constant reminder to any who would try to capture the Spirit in any box—whether the offender be a denomination, crusade, movement, or gift of the Spirit. The Spirit goes where he will.

Tongues appear in Acts 2 as miracles. Jewish pilgrims had gathered in Jerusalem from all over the Empire, having come from many nations with differing language backgrounds. What amazed them about these tongues was that each of the pilgrims was able to understand everyone else in their own dialects (v. 8). Luke certainly intended to communicate a miracle of *hearing*. The emphasis is on the gift of the Spirit. Tongues are incidental to the story.

Only twice outside chapter 2 are tongues mentioned in

Acts. They receive passing mention in 10:46 and 19:6. In each of these cases the emphasis is upon the power of the Spirit, with tongues mentioned as only one manifestation of the Spirit's presence. It is clear that tongues are not a continuing emphasis in Acts. What is most important is that the presence of the Spirit was with the early church as it broke barriers.

This presence is nowhere more clearly emphasized than in the letters of Paul. Paul was very clear in his view of the Holy Spirit as a valuable and distinct person in the Godhead. This distinction is sharply seen in the benediction in 2 Corinthians 13:13.

Paul often spoke of the Holy Spirit as related to and identical with the two other persons of the Godhead. In Romans 8:9 Paul said, "The Spirit of God dwells in you . . . . If any man have not the Spirit of Christ, he is none of his." Second Corinthians 3:17 reads, "Now the Lord is that Spirit; and where the Spirit of the Lord is, there is liberty."

For Paul, the continuing process of sanctification was affected by the Spirit of God (1 Cor. 6:11). In this process, the whole church is being redeemed and cleansed. What takes place in the church also takes place in the individual, and vice versa. Emil Brunner describes sanctification as that process in which the Holy Spirit of God claims back for himself every aspect of the believer's personality. This winning by the Spirit allows the harmony of the body of believers to develop. This is a warning to any person tempted to disrupt the fellowship of God's church.

So it is clear that Paul saw the Spirit of God as glorifying Christ as he operates in and through believers, alone and in the church. In such work, the Holy Spirit builds up the church and gives it power for witness and ministry. This is made clear in 2 Corinthians 3:3, in which Paul said that believers are letters "written not with ink but with the Spirit of the living God" (RSV).

The book of Hebrews adds valuable insights into the work of the Spirit. The gifts are mentioned in passing in 2:4. The Spirit is presented as inspiring the Old Testament in 3:7–19 and 9:8. (This was quite a chronological leap backward and theological leap forward for the first Jewish readers of Hebrews.) In 9:14, the author of this epistle presented Christ's going to the cross in the "eternal Spirit." In 6:4, believers are urged to be "partakers with the Holy Spirit" (RSV).

Revelation closes the canon with frequent mentions of the Holy Spirit. In fact, the visions themselves are presented as a result of John's being "in the Spirit on the Lord's day" (1:10, RSV). It was the Spirit who spoke through John to the seven churches of Asia (2:7; 3:6). The Bible closes as it began, with a continuing emphasis on the Holy Spirit. Revelation 22:17 reads, "The Spirit and the bride say, Come . . . . And whosoever will, let him take the water of life freely."

As can be seen clearly, the Bible has a lot to say about the Holy Spirit. He is present from beginning to end as constantly empowering and strengthening persons. He leads to the truth because he is the truth, as is the Son. He is part of the fabric of life, for indeed he is the breath of life. He came at Pentecost as part of a continuing drama, not a one-act play. His work flows as does the power of God, interacting with the entirety of human history. Among believers the Spirit empowers, enables, and creates unity with Christ and with each other. He lives and invites

THE SPIRIT IN SEARCH OF A BIBLICAL THEOLOGY   35

within those whose life-style bespeak his presence.

Within this total context of fellowship, two areas of controversy still linger on between Pentecostals and non-Pentecostals. Worthy of consideration are the "baptism of the Spirit" and "speaking in tongues."

"Baptism in the Spirit" is part and parcel of the new Pentecostalism. The reasoning goes like this:

1. Baptism in water and baptism in the Spirit are two separate occurrences.

2. Conversion is the sinner's acceptance of Jesus, which brings salvation. Here can be seen the repentant sinner as the object of God's salvation.

3. The Lord is not satisfied with conversion alone.

4. So, a second time we are confronted with God.

5. This second confrontation is called "baptism in the Spirit." Through it the Christian is brought into a *deeper* relationship with Christ.

6. The believer is therefore now not an object, but an instrument of salvation.

7. The result of this second baptism is accompanying gifts and powers. (Acts 8:14–16 is frequently cited as an example of this idea.)

8. As in Acts 19:2, part of the work of the early apostles was to bring the baptism of the Spirit to every Christian. In that verse they asked, "Did you receive the Holy Spirit when you believed?" (RSV).

These claims are built on a limited understanding of salvation. The root word means wholeness. It is a contradiction in terms to maintain that one is half-saved at conversion or is incomplete without a "second work of grace." Separation of the baptisms does injustice to Acts 2:38, where no such separation is indicated in the text.

Salvation is a continuing relationship between God and the repentant sinner.

At all stages of salvation, the believer is both object and instrument. As was Israel in the Old Testament, the groups of believers in the new Israel are both recipients and sharers of grace. The total biblical witness is to the unity of the works of the persons of the Trinity. To separate them at the critical time of salvation is to fragment both the believer and the bringers of salvation—the Father, the Son, and the Holy Spirit. This explanation helps to account for the fact that it was generally assumed in the early church that to receive Christ was to receive the Spirit. That is why Acts 19:2 is a record of one of a few isolated incidents in which early apostles asked such a question.

The report of such an occurrence does not make it a central requirement for spiritual growth. The Spirit was frequently invoked to begin a missionary journey. This does not imply that those about to embark did not already have both the Son and the Spirit. The Spirit was prayed upon them that they might be continually effective in their witness. They were already both object and spreader of God's salvation through the Father, Son, and Spirit.

In Colossians 2:9–10 Paul was arguing that the Colossians did not need any additional savior figures. They, after all, already had Christ; and not only "in him the whole fulness of the deity dwells bodily," but they themselves "have come to fulness of life in him" (RSV). Paul was not referring to a second experience but to the Christian baptism that all the believers have in common.

The New Testament contains no records of believers in Christ who did not become baptized. This is because the

THE SPIRIT IN SEARCH OF A BIBLICAL THEOLOGY 37

word *baptizo* is associated with repentance, entry into the kingdom, forgiveness of sins, reception of the Spirit, and union with Christ in his death and risen life. Baptism is the work of the new life and reception of the Spirit of Christ.

Baptism is incorporation into Christ, so it is not to be seen as the bare external rite. Baptism is a conglomerate word in the New Testament, including incorporation into Christ and reception of the Spirit.

There are three strands entering into the process of salvation from the beginning. The human side is repentance and faith. The divine side is reception of the Holy Spirit, reception into the family of God, and forgiveness of sins. The churchly part is acceptance into a body of believers. To separate them chronologically or theologically is to destroy their unity.

So what are Bible believers to do with those passages in Acts that speak of two baptisms?

First, it is important to note that Luke, the author of Acts, did not supply us with a theology of Christian initiation. Sometimes for him reception of the Spirit followed baptism (Acts 2:8 ff.). Sometimes baptism is preceded by reception of the Spirit (Acts 10:44 ff.); and sometimes a person is baptized who has no part in the Christian way at all. His heart may still be directed toward wickedness (Acts 8:21). If any Bible student is looking to Acts for a pattern of baptism or reception of the Spirit, he looks in vain.

The events of Acts 19 are clearly presented as isolated happenings. Paul asked a handful of disciples, "Did you receive the Holy Spirit when you believed?" (v. 2, RSV).

Acts 19 goes on to make it clear that these disciples were in no sense Christians. They had been baptized by John the Baptist (v. 3) and then had gone away to Ephesus. They even had to be informed by Paul that the Coming One whom John the Baptist predicted was in fact Jesus of Nazareth. So they had never heard of Jesus, much less believed in him or been baptized in his name.

Incidentally, they were also quite uninformed about the Holy Spirit. He was just part of the whole package they had never opened or even received. These disciples of John the Baptist said, "We have never even heard that there is a Holy Spirit" (v. 2, RSV). These disciples were baptized in the name of the Lord Jesus, and they received the Spirit—at the same time.

Acts 8 is problematical. Philip preached to the Samaritans, and hundreds responded. Demons were cast out; the lame were healed. Peter and John then came up *from Jerusalem* to see what was going on. This made the Samaritan adventure an extension of the Jerusalem church, an event recorded by Luke to emphasize further spreading of the gospel. In John 4:9 we read, "The Jews have no dealings with the Samaritans." Apostles came to Samaria from Jerusalem to mark their solidarity with the new converts. Luke was emphasizing the solidarity of the rapidly spreading young church.

There are, indeed, very few references in the New Testament to "baptism in the Holy Spirit." There are only seven such references, and six of them refer to the baptism that John the Baptist promised that the Coming One would bring (Mark 1:8; Luke 3:16; Matt. 3:11; John 1:33; Acts 1:5; 11:16). There is a very clear picture presented here. John baptized with water to mark repentance. Jesus will baptize with the Holy Spirit to bring persons into the blessings of the New Covenant.

THE SPIRIT IN SEARCH OF A BIBLICAL THEOLOGY 39

The other reference is 1 Corinthians 12:13. Paul was very clear here. He said, "By one Spirit we were all baptized into one body . . . and all were made to drink of one Spirit" (RSV). He was saying that it is the One Spirit who baptizes believers into the one body of Christ. The Spirit of God brings persons into the family of God, and it is foolish to speak of the Spirit as baptizing believers—persons who already have the Spirit.

All believers are adopted into God's family and are recipients of the Holy Spirit. To describe a second experience for those who are already Christians is contrary to the general thrust of the New Testament witness. (See chap. 3 for an in-depth discussion of the second major controversy spurred by the neo-Pentecostal movement, speaking in tongues.)

All of this is not to deny that thousands of believers today operate in a lukewarm blandness they manage to label Christian. The Spirit and the Son await the receptivity of the repentant sinners who have already begun the Christian pilgrimage but who are still babes. That is the importance of what Scripture references call being "filled with the Spirit."

Ephesians 5:18 says, "Be not drunk with wine, wherein is excess; but be filled with the Spirit." "Be filled" in that verse is an imperative. The believer does not have to wonder whether it is the thing to do. It is a mandate and is carried out through continuing action. This verb, meaning "fill to overflowing," is *plerousthé*, which refers to an enduring action.

The command is for the Christian to "keep on being filled to overflowing" with the Spirit. The experience is even more continual than being filled again and again.

The command is to be filled in nonstop action. It should also be noted that the verb is in the passive voice. The Spirit acts upon the believer because the believer remains willing and open.

There is a qualitative difference in the Bible between the constant filling of the Spirit (which is commanded) and "the baptism of the Spirit," which is referred to in a nonsystematic fashion. A constant state of openness to the powerful Spirit is to be desired above argumentation about whether one is baptized once into Christ and again into the Spirit.

First Corinthians 12—15 is Paul's advice to that little colony of heaven in a specific situation in the wicked, first-century city of Corinth. In these four chapters we are face to face with a serious spiritual problem. Corinth and its fledgling church are hardly to be emulated, although Paul's advice is certainly to be taken seriously.

The underlying question for chapters 12—15 is "Who is truly spiritual?" Paul, in his typical polemical style, began in verse 2 by reminding his readers what true spirituality is not. Here he was saying that the truly spiritual one is *not* one swept away in ecstasy. So Paul was dealing with tongues as a problem, not as a sign of excellence. He was trying to control a problem, not to recommend tongues.

First Corinthians 12:3 is a gentle reminder to any who would seek to separate the work of Jesus from the role of the Spirit. The person who confesses "Jesus is Lord," for Paul, has experienced already the deep work of the Spirit. This work of the Spirit is to use the ego Christocentrically. The Spirit does not replace, wipe out, remove, or overpower the ego.

Paul was setting the stage for the remainder of these

THE SPIRIT IN SEARCH OF A BIBLICAL THEOLOGY 41

four chapters. He was saying, "Before you confessed that Jesus is Lord, you were swept away by spiritual forces that did not belong to him. Now, you have the *Holy* Spirit who is one with the Jesus you confess as Lord."

In verses 1,4–7, Paul began to discuss the "spiritual gifts." (Note that unity in the Spirit is stressed through this section.)

The gifts listed here have five characteristics. They are:

1. *Thanerosa*—"manifestations" (v. 7). They are visible graces that are seen or heard or felt. Thereby God is glorified in his Spirit.

2. *Energemata*—"varieties of working" (v. 6, RSV). As such, these gifts are momentary powers and not permanent endowments. They are, in modern parlance, bursts of spiritual "energy." (Note the Greek word.)

3. *Diakoniai*—"services" (v. 5, RSV). The gifts are for the purpose of ministry. The object is to help *others,* not to build up any one individual.

4. *Charismata*—grace "gifts" (v. 4). These manifestations are gifts, not rewards for righteousness. Therefore, they are not sources of false pride. Again, the Spirit goes where he will.

5. *Pneumatika*—"spiritual" (v. 1). Literally, verse 1 should be read, "Now concerning the spirituals . . ." As such, these are gifts *of the Spirit* and do not come as a result of natural abilities. They come in spite of any ranking any church may have to measure worthiness.

Throughout Paul's discussion of these gifts, it is clear that the work of the Spirit is the honoring of Jesus. Paul tried to preserve the living inner relationship of the Spirit to and for Christ. Therefore, these gifts are all "for the common good."

In verses 8–11, Paul listed some of the gifts he had in mind. Listed first, purposefully, is the gift of understandable speech. Listed last, pointedly, is the gift of unintelligible speech.

Paul viewed these gifts from the important perspective of the body of Christ. So he did not value any gift for its own sake, but for the sake of the upbuilding of the body. A gift could hardly exist, in Paul's thinking, unless it existed for the church. For example, tongues are valuable only if they are interpreted for the congregation.

Because Paul understood the basic work of the Spirit to be the honoring of Christ, it is no wonder that he saw the work of the "grace-gifted" to be in the service of Christ's body.

In verses 12–13, Paul argued that just as there are arms, legs, and organs in a single body, to be unique does not endanger the body's unity.

In verse 13, Paul came closer to saying "baptism in the Holy Spirit" than anywhere else in his writings. Even here, the phrase is used to stress once again the oneness of Christians in the present context. Paul used the event of baptism as a symbolic reminder of the Christians' unity. "*All* of you have been baptized together into Christ," Paul argued. Paul was here certainly not teaching an unusual spirit baptism won only by a few, but the grace-filled baptism through the Spirit given freely to *all* believers.

The great word of this entire chapter 12 is *one*. There are not, for Paul, two bodies of Christian believers: one filled with nominal Christians into which all are baptized in water, and another filled with spiritual belief into which deeper Christians are baptized in the Spirit. So, as is evident in verse 13, the baptism of the Holy Spirit and the baptism of the believer into Christ are one. Baptism into the body of Christ is *not* a spirit-deprived matter to be upgraded later by a so-called spiritual baptism into the Spirit. The Spirit gives himself at baptism in the fullness of Christ.

There must have been a note of sadness in Paul's heart when he rebuked the Corinthians for being unspiritual in spite of the fact that they were baptized, gifted, and filled by the Spirit.

In verses 14–31 of chapter 12, Paul felt free to speak of the variety of gifts, having spoken passionately of the oneness of the Spirit. While there are varieties of gifts, no one is to feel inferior or superior because of his own gifts. In verse 18 it is clear that God has chosen in his free will to arrange the parts of the body. Every part of the body is therefore free to admit its obvious need for the others.

In 1 Corinthians 13 every statement is categorical. There is no room for argument. In this chapter Paul connected spiritual things with love. Paul said here that without love all the "grace gifts" are dis-graced.

In verse 1, for example, Paul stated that the supremacy of love over the gift of tongues is evident. The Corinthians had a weakness for brilliance, but Paul here insisted that love is more than eloquence.

The following verse indicates that love is superior to the gift of inspired preaching and teaching. A clear head is of no significance for the believer without a loving heart.

Verse 4 contains Paul's definition of Christian love, in which he called love *makrothumei*—that is, "making broad." Christian love is not so momentary as enduring.

Verse 5 is crucial because it describes Christian love as "seek[ing] not her own." Likewise, the grace gifts are given to the service of the body of Christ into which they have been baptized. There is no false "higher" way of the Spirit which supersedes the way of love.

First Corinthians 14 is a continuation of Paul's arguments. He has described a love life-style in the poem of love. Now Paul prayed in prose that Christ's people would follow after love with the same zeal they had when they searched for the thrill of the Spirit's presence.

Paul valued grace gifts for their ability to help persons within the body. Therefore, tongues are not to be especially glorified because they have the inherent weakness of being directed to God, who needs no building up. In verse 4 Paul did *not* deny that tongues are gifts, but he did not direct the Corinthians to *seek* tongues. Paul did not despise the gift of tongues. In fact, he said in verse 5 that tongues *could* be useful when aided by the grace gift of interpretation. The key consideration continues to be the building up of the body.

Verses 20–25 serve as Paul's reminder that the gifts could blur a key function of the church, which is evangelism. In verse 23, Paul argued that nonbelievers could think that tongue speakers were crazy or drunk. On the other hand, testimonies (prophecy) have an inherent missionary power about them. Paul thought that the public use of grace gifts should be considered seriously on the basis of their potential effect on evangelistic efforts.

In verses 26–33 of chapter 14, Paul began to summarize by discussing a church meeting. *Each* is a key word in the sense of corporate participation in worship. Again, Paul did not advise against the use of tongues. He did give three qualifications, however:

1. Not more than three persons;

THE SPIRIT IN SEARCH OF A BIBLICAL THEOLOGY 45

2. One at a time;
3. With an interpreter.

For those who would seek to deal with tongues by labeling them demonic, a question immediately arises: Would Paul have described as a gift anything which was inherently demonic? The practice of quick-labeling is a cop-out in dealing with this complex issue. (Note also that prophets should also speak in turn.)

Verse 29 is translated in The New English Bible as "While the rest exercise their judgment upon what is said." This interpretation makes it very clear that the mind is not to be shifted into neutral while the Spirit operates.

Those Christians currently in formal, traditional churches should note that Paul's picture of worship here is one in which several gifts were demonstrated by several believers. There was implied a free-flowing opportunity for Spirit-filled believers to worship as part of the service by displaying their respective gifts. Evidently a group discussion followed the various presentations. The ministry was a shared one. There was a prominent place given to a thought-filled conversational format. This is a valuable lesson for all churches to learn from Pentecostalism, old or new.

In the concluding verses, 39-40, Paul gave a plea for testimony to prevail. But, as he made clear, tongues are not to be forbidden. His concern for the upbuilding of the body shone through. He trusted that love would prevail so that the grace gifts could glorify the graceful Lord from whom they came.

Wait a minute! Do not stop here! Chapter 15 is a part of this four-chapter unit for Paul and the Corinthians. As the

Corinthians sought to separate the spiritual from the unspiritual in the case of gifts, they also wanted to divide the spirit from the flesh in the future resurrection. In both cases, there was a despising of the fleshly body. This gave room for an overestimation of the value of the Spirit. This unbalanced piety created a number of problems for the Corinthians.

Paul began chapter 15 by bragging on Jesus and his gospel. The Spirit is important as he brings *unity* in Christ. Paul would stand for no truncated theology that separates the Holy Spirit from Christ or the flesh from the Spirit. The believer will one day be raised in unity as he now believes in the unity created by the Spirit. The continuing theme is unity.

In summary, for Paul, there were three criteria for determining whether a movement is of the Spirit. They are:

1. Does it glorify the person of Jesus? It follows that Spirit-filled Christians who virtually ignore the work and value of Christ should beware of imbalance.

2. Does it help persons? Some who are claiming to be Spirit-filled are ignoring the social needs of persons in secular society and/or believers in the body. Paul would stand for no such division of the Spirit.

3. Is it thematically true to the Word? To select one verse or instance in the Bible out of context is to do injustice to the total biblical witness. The thrust of the biblical record is that Jesus and the Spirit are one with the Father. To separate them at baptism or later in the body is to tear at the roots of the written witness.

This third point is particularly relevant because most charismatics claim to take the Bible seriously, if not literally.

No serious student of the Bible can ignore the fact that the Spirit brought freedom to the church of the first century. These same serious students, while perhaps not doubting the beauty and freedom the Spirit brings, have reason to doubt some "scriptural" reasons given for that experience.

Charismatic Christians on the whole tend to be highly selective in their approach to Scripture. Encountering the Spirit in a series of personal experiences, some new Pentecostals thereafter come to see the Word in the light of those experiences. The Bible judges experience, not the opposite. Judging Scripture by experience allows some new Pentecostals to concentrate on Acts to the neglect of John or the Corinthian correspondence or Ephesians.

The overwhelming evidence of the New Testament is that all Christians have the Spirit upon belief in Jesus. To be sure, many Christians experience a life-giving encounter with the Spirit after belief in the Son. For that, all believers can rejoice. "Being biblical" involves the total written Word, not building a whole practice on isolated texts. Bible students may therefore legitimately give a reminder to some of the new Pentecostals that in seeking to be biblically based, all the Word is to be viewed as it judges all of us.

New Pentecostals will have to give serious answers to those who charge the Pentecostal exegetical methods with several weaknesses, including:

1. Concentration on three occurrences in Acts (chaps. 2,8,19) does not a canon make.

2. Paul's placement of testimony above tongues in 1 Corinthians is to be tempered with love.

3. Insistence upon a "second baptism" is difficult to substantiate in light of the total New Testament's emphasis on the unity of the Spirit and the Son.

4. Laying particular emphasis upon the nine gifts of the Spirit listed in 1 Corinthians 12 only takes care of part of the total picture. In fact, a compiling of the multiple lists of gifts as recorded in New Testament letters reveals not nine but at least seventeen grace gifts. (See Rom. 12:6–8; 1 Cor. 12:9–10, 28–30; Eph. 4:11–16.)

The total scriptural witness sheds light on itself. In its totality, it sheds valuable light on any issue or set of concerns. It is imperative that both new Pentecostals and non-Pentecostals judge their discipleship by the Word and not by other means. If both heed the Word, needed dialogue between the two groups may occur. This sharing will be crippled, however, as long as either group insists on using its respective and selective canon within the canon.

Conclusion

From start to finish, the Bible is inspired by and concerned with the Holy Spirit. His unity with the Father and Son is stressed so often that it can only be called tragedy when the Spirit seemingly divides Bible believers.

With this reminder in the background, it is important that the new Pentecostalism be viewed intelligently in light of Scripture. Anyone conversing with an individual or group within the new Pentecostalism will command attention when he speaks in love from the Word.

That discussion is overdue.

3. Tongues of Change

One of the most controversial aspects of the new Pentecostal movement is the question of speaking in tongues. Many of the new Pentecostals, though certainly not all, insist that tongues-speaking is the key sign marking the reception of the baptism of the Spirit. One of those who does so is Don Basham, a popular author among new Pentecostals. He writes in *A Handbook on Holy Spirit Baptism:* "The only clear scriptural evidence of the baptism of the Holy Spirit is speaking in tongues . . . . The unique evidence that the 120 (at Pentecost) received the Holy Spirit was that 'they began to speak in other tongues' (Acts 2:4)."

To supply that scriptural evidence, Mr. Basham states that Acts records five separate occasions when the Holy Spirit was received and that on three of these occasions tongues are mentioned (Acts 2:4; 10:44 ff.; 19:6).[1]

Mr. Basham later defines tongues as "a form of prayer in which the Christian yields himself to the Holy Spirit and receives from the Spirit a super-natural language with which to praise God."[2]

There are many reasons given by new Pentecostals for speaking in tongues. None has stated the case so strongly as Henry Noss in a booklet entitled "The Baptism with the Holy Spirit," in which he lists twenty reasons—each with a

Scripture verse to support it. (They are listed here as information, even for the non-Pentecostal who seeks knowledge of what makes his neo-Pentecostal neighbor think and behave as he does.) They are:

1. Speaking with tongues is the *unique* spiritual gift identified with the church (Acts 2:4).

2. It was ordained by God for the church (1 Cor. 12:28).

3. It is a specific fulfillment of prophecy (Joel 2:28).

4. It is a sign *of* the believer (John 7:38–39).

5. It is a sign *to* the unbeliever (1 Cor. 14:22).

6. It is a proof of the resurrection of Jesus Christ (John 16:7).

7. It is an evidence of the baptism of the Holy Spirit (Acts 19:6).

8. It is a means of preaching to men of other languages (Acts 2:6 ff.).

9. It is a spiritual gift for self-edification (1 Cor. 14:4).

10. It is a gift for the spiritual edification of the church (1 Cor. 14:5).

11. It is a gift for communicating with God in private worship (1 Cor. 14:2).

12. It is a means by which the Holy Spirit intercedes through us in prayer (Rom. 8:26).

13. It is a gift for singing in the spirit (Eph. 5:18–19).

14. Paul was thankful for the privilege (1 Cor. 14:18).

15. Paul desired that all would speak in tongues (1 Cor. 14:5).

16. Speaking in tongues is one of the gifts of the Spirit (1 Cor. 12:10).

17. Paul ordered that it not be forbidden (1 Cor. 14:39).

18. Isaiah referred to it as a "rest" (Isa. 28:12).

19. Isaiah referred to it as "refreshing" (Isa. 28:12).

20. It follows as a confirmation of the Word of God when it is preached (Mark 16:17).[3]

Of course, it is immediately apparent that little biblical criticism is used in the list above. For example, Mark 16 is quoted without reference to its being from a later addition to that gospel. Further, it should be noted that the word tongues is used by Mr. Noss indiscriminately, as if there were no distinction between its uses in Isaiah, Acts, and 1 Corinthians. Nonetheless, this is a summary of the reasons given for speaking in tongues by new Pentecostals.

Oral Roberts, very popular among the new Pentecostals, wrote a book with the lengthy title *The Baptism with the Holy Spirit and the Value of Speaking in Tongues Today*. In it he argues that tongues are needed today for two simple reasons:

1. There is the need in a group of believers for edification.
2. Interpretation of diverse kinds of tongues provides the edification needed.[4]

This pre-new Pentecostal argument actually provides only one of the numerous reasons given by new Pentecostals for speaking in tongues. After the rise of neo-Pentecostalism and his change of involvement from traditional Pentecostal to mainline Methodist university president, Mr. Roberts has become more cautious. He told an overflow audience in Atlanta in 1974, "Healing does not reside in me, but in the Spirit. If you put all the gifts of the Spirit in a circle and put Jesus Christ in the center, then you will see the gifts as extensions of Jesus Christ. They have no existence outside Christ." [5]

While most new Pentecostals seem intent on experiencing and enjoying tongues, no end of analysis goes on when one tries to dissect what this phenomenon is. From within and without the movement, analysis continues.

It is becoming clearer to both participants in and observers of tongues-speaking that no one analytical apparatus will do to explain completely this complex series of happenings. Failure to communicate continues partly because persons on both sides of the tongues issue continue to analyze this complexity from only one or two angles. Yet, tongues are so complex that they must be viewed in their totality of divine-human interaction to be understood at all.

At least eight perspectives merit attention in explaining and understanding tongues. They are (perhaps in order of importance): biblical, theological, historical (from a "History of Religions" approach), linguistic, psychological, sociological (as in group dynamic), and anthropological. Each of these will be taken in turn.

1. The Biblical.—The New Testament varies in its references to tongues. In English, no one team should or can do to express such varied words as: "new tongues" (Mark 16:17), "other tongues" (Acts 2:4), "tongues" (Acts 19:6), and "kinds of tongues" (1 Cor. 12:10).

Within the letter called 1 Corinthians itself, there are three distinct labels for tongues. They are "kinds of tongues" (12:10), "tongues" (12:30), and "interpretation of tongues" (12:10). The matter of tongues is thus seen to be more complex than the mere repetition of the English word tongues.

Frank Stagg gives some help regarding *glossolalia*. In his study of the Greek word for "tongue," *glossa*, he points out that it is used in the literal sense (tongue) more often than not in the New Testament. There are two other ways it is used, however: for language itself (Rev. 5:9) and for strange or obscure speech (Acts 2:3).[6]

One can easily see that what was going on in Luke's, Paul's, and John's minds when they used the word *glossa* was quite different. In Acts 2, Luke was describing a miracle of hearing at an event in which a tongue was spoken, and *everyone* understood. Paul was speaking to a problem situation in Corinth in which a person was speaking in a tongue which *none* understood, except perhaps an interpreter. John was using the word in Revelation to depict a new day in which persons of many tongues would bow at the feet of Jesus.

At least one implication of the biblical study of tongues is that the term cannot be used indiscriminately, whether in an academic seminar or a neighborhood prayer meeting.

This explanation is further complicated by the fact that new Pentecostals, in everyday enjoyment of their response to the Spirit, use tongues to refer to three distinct types of experiences. One of these is "singing in the spirit" (Eph. 5:18–19). Another is mild and rather quiet praise given near the beginning of a prayer meeting, sometimes called the "warm-up" period. Again, there is the "new tongue" or "sign tongue" given at initiation through the baptism of the spirit.

Chapters 12—15 in 1 Corinthians give many practical hints regarding tongues. Many of those have been covered in the previous chapter. One that was not covered deserves some attention here. In 14:34 of that section, Paul made it clear that tongues are to be reserved for the use of men. Women were to "keep silent." This is one of the controls Paul placed over the use of tongues, one that must be dealt with openly by the neo-Pentecostals. Within their number, the female participants predominate—but do not dominate.

Further, it is easy to see that for Paul, tongues constituted the *least* of the gifts. He elevated prophecy, or intelligent speech in testimony, above tongues. This chart makes this obvious:

Tongues

1. Speaks to God (14:2).
2. Shows immaturity (14:20).
3. Confirms the skepticism of a nonbeliever (14:2).
4. Often uncontrolled (14:14).
5. Edifies only the individual unless there is an interpreter (14:4).

Prophecy

1. Speaks to men (14:2).
2. Expresses maturity (14:20).
3. Leads to the conviction of a nonbeliever (14:24).
4. Controlled by the prophet (14:32).
5. Edifies the whole church (14:4).

In any case, the ruling factor is to be love, the highest kind of patient love that God gives to churches willing to receive and use it. It is his highest gift.

2. *The Theological.*—The Bible sets the tone for all theology, including that of tongues. At least three major theological themes evolve out of the study of tongues with a biblical base (including what was done in the previous chapter). They are:

A. No one person in the Trinity should be allowed to

TONGUES OF CHANGE

predominate in a maturing Christian pilgrimage. Speaking in tongues as a sign of being baptized in the Spirit is not superior to a salvation experience with Christ or a continuing relationship with the loving Father. No one experience can dissect the Trinity or elevate any one person within it as giving more access to discipleship than either of the other two.

B. *Glossolalia* and *tongues-speaking* should not be used interchangeably and without reference to biblical context. God works in mysterious ways and may choose, specifically through his Spirit, to work with any part of the body as he chooses. In any outpouring of the Spirit the tongue may be used as a witness, as an instrument to bring about a miracle of hearing or as a means by which listening to an unknown tongue can be turned into a meaningful utterance for an entire group in worship. To try to force an experience of speaking in tongues on a disciple is to miss part of the point of God's versatility in his work and world. To forbid the use of tongues is to go to the other extreme.

C. Tongues are for the express purpose of building up the fellowship of the body of Christ. When they become divisive, a reconsideration has to be given to their use and certainly to an insistence of their use. Conversely, those out of tune with the general principle of being open to the gifts of the Spirit should analyze whether it is their lack of openness that makes tongues divisive.

3. The Historical.—This is certainly not the first generation of disciples to find tongues-speaking a subject of controversy. There was, in fact, a group present in Corinth at the time of Paul's letters. They were called Gnostics and divided persons into three categories: the true believers capable of receiving a secret knowledge, those capable of receiving "mere" salvation, and those who would always remain inattentive to the Spirit. Tongues were common among the true Gnostics and were seen as a sure sign of that superior category.

Martin Luther, an instigator of the Protestant Reformation, wrote that each believer might expect to receive one or more gifts of the Spirit as a sign of the true church.

John Calvin argued that God had removed tongues from the church rather than have them abused as they had been in Corinth.

John Wesley, the founder of Methodism, knew that tongues were frequently given as a sign of the Spirit during his day. He stated that God for some reason had not seen fit to give that gift to him.

In the 1830s a new American sect emerged. The members followed Joseph Smith, Jr. (1805-1844), and were called Mormons. Smith wrote, "We believe in the gift of tongues, prophecy, etc."

Brigham Young started praying in tongues a few weeks after his baptism. Joseph Smith proclaimed that the gift of tongues was "the pure Adamic language." *The Book of Mormon* (9:7) states that deniers of these gifts "know not the gospel." It is, therefore, quite to be expected that the first Mormon constitution stated, "We believe in the gift of tongues, prophecy, . . . etc." [7]

Modern Mormons seldom exhibit these gifts. I once spoke with an elderly Mormon mission pioneer to the Netherlands, who told me that in the 1930s the Mormons "had a lot of trouble" with tongues there but that he had not heard them much since then. This was in spite of the fact that he had visited or supervised Mormon mission work in more than a dozen nations since the 1930s.

TONGUES OF CHANGE

(This poses a problem for those neo-Pentecostals who argue that tongues-speaking is a sign of a true believer in Christ. Doctrinally, Mormonism represents a wide deviance from mainline Christian expression. Can one be doctrinally inconsistent and Spirit-filled? Or can one insist upon tenets of faith widely divergent from mainline Christianity and still be of the Spirit?)

The neo-Pentecostal movement of the late 1970s is not the first or the last time God will pour out his Spirit on weak disciples unable to respond in balance to him. That historical perspective is important because of the narrow "now" vision with which the issues are being debated now.

4. The "History of Religions" Approach.—"History of Religions" was popularized at the University of Chicago as a fancy way of saying the study of the entirety of religious expression, especially as seen in its historical context.

The wider study of religion reveals the almost universal use of tongues among mystical persons in every age, clime, and doctrinal setting. The ecstasy of unintelligible speech was quite common in the Greek mystery religions. One such mind-set was Orphism, which saw man as a mixture of immortal soul and limited body. Therefore, ecstasy was used as a method to get that soul outside the limits of the body. Ecstatic speech was a sign of that escape.

Something similar was going on in Corinth when Paul wrote to the struggling Christians there. The Christians were conditioned to experience tongues before they became Christians. They were borrowing a pre-Christian form of expression. (Again, there is an obvious problem here for those who insist that tongues are a sure sign of the Holy Spirit.)

Further back in history, there was a running controversy between prophets in the Old Testament era, who argued about whether a prophet should engage in ecstatic utterances. Especially among the earlier Hebrew prophets, there were those who whirled themselves into a frenzy and then spoke in spiritual manner (1 Sam. 10:5 ff. and 2 Sam. 6:13 ff.).

Islam is Christianity's major competitor in terms of number of adherents. Within the Moslem family there are the Sufis, mystics who seek a higher form of loving knowledge by practicing many exercises to induce that knowledge. The Sufi dancers are known worldwide and are called whirling dervishes because of their frantic dances. These dances produce, after three or four hours of nonstop action, a type of unintelligible speech called tongues.

The animistic world is filled with healers who whip themselves into ecstatic frenzy before they prophesy and recommend healing devices. Foretelling the future, divination, healing, and blessing the community—all traditional roles of the shaman—are all done with tongues on occasion.

(For a thorough review of this topic, see L. Carlyle May, "A Survey of Glossolalia and Related Phenomena in Non-Christian Religions." [8]

Any consideration of tongues must therefore be done on the basis of the full knowledge that they are found almost universally in religious expression. Tongues are not a uniquely Christian occurrence.

5. *The Linguistic.*—Reports persist among neo-Pentecostals that at times one who is speaking in tongues begins to speak fluently in a known language, such as

Japanese, although he knows no Japanese at all. Don Basham and others see this as a continuing miracle.

However, Eugene A. Nida, secretary of translations for the American Bible Society, has analyzed dozens of tape-recorded experiences of tongues from all over the world and has concluded that they lack certain elements of a true language.[9]

Linguistic analysis of a typical tongues session indicates sounds being made which have dominant vowel sounds and a high degree of repetition. Tongues sound like any language in which there are almost as many vowels as consonants, such as the Melanesian family of languages.

A printout of a tongues session would contain sounds like:

"Vole virte vom";

"Imba, imba, imba"; *or*

"Elee, lete, leele, lotu."

6. *The Psychological.*—Morton T. Kelsey, in *Tongue Speaking*, drew a psychological profile of the person most likely to be a tongues speaker. He found that person to be an extrovert, one who is concerned about his world and in whom there is a high sense of value. He may have been inhibited in constructive outlets of that value-motivated concern.[10]

Erik Erikson paints a far less complimentary picture, one of the type of person whose communications outlets have been blocked. His findings may be paraphrased as concluding that it is no wonder that persons whose religious strivings are suppressed through sophistication institutionalization and a very superficial social behavior will suddenly break into tongues.[11] In plain language, the one who is bottled-up at home, on the job, or at church is a most likely candidate to speak in tongues when the opportunity comes.

Even a casual observation of the new Pentecostal movement reveals that here is a group with a high number of women and youth involved. Few bishops among the clergy get involved. Among evangelicals, the pastors most likely to get involved are those pastoring small churches in a fringe area, geographically speaking, of their group's traditional areas of dominance. What do these persons have in common? They are the disenfranchised, those without power bases in our society. Are tongues being used to compensate with an exchange of spiritual elitism for a feeling of powerlessness? Undoubtedly, in some cases.

A broad generalization, however, which sees the tongues-speaker as some kind of weird person full of psychotic or social needs, is grossly unfair. The new Pentecostal also may be the local financier and member of the city council who is fifty years old and in the center of political, economic, and spiritual power. At any rate, the Spirit goes where he will. Those outside traditional sources of power may be just more open to that going.

Many Christians still look down on the Pentecostal as a neurotic, insecure person who can express himself only in unconventional ways or forms of speech. But some psychological tests have indicated that the opposite may be true. In many cases, it has been found, the gifts seem to contribute to mental health.

7. *The Sociological.*—There are factors in the group dynamic that usually surround the first occasion of tongues for the initiate into neo-Pentecostalism. The group is usually characterized by a deep sense of commitment to each

other and exhibits an obvious spirit of acceptance. In short, it is the kind of group most persons would want to be a part of.

When tongues are being induced by the group (again, this is *not* true of all neo-Pentecostals), there is likely to be a fever-pitch type of emotional atmosphere. At this stage, a leader comes into play. He or she tells the potential tongues speaker to hold nothing back. There is to be complete trust in the group leader as well as in the Lord.

This trust may be accompanied, in some cases, by severe group pressure. I attended a Full Gospel Businessmen's Fellowship luncheon at the luxurious Hyatt Regency Hotel in Atlanta in May, 1974. After the luncheon, those interested in knowing more about "baptism in the Spirit" were asked to stay for an "after meeting" in a smaller side room. A young businessman indicated to the group leader that he had never been baptized of the Spirit or spoken in tongues, and he would certainly like to.

At this, the leader had the young man take off his coat, loosen his tie, and kneel before the leader. The initiate was instructed to shake his head rapidly, let his jaw drop, and let his tongue be loose. Then five or six men placed their hands on his head and let go simultaneously. When this failed once and was repeated, the young man did begin to speak in unintelligible words.

The group dynamic is a definite factor in experiencing for the first time in most cases. The positive qualities of group acceptance are mingled with inducement to "feel the Spirit." No study of tongues ignoring the strong group influence is complete.

8. *The Anthropological.*—"Rites of passage" are known well to students of anthropology. They are ceremonies which mark important events in the lives of all individuals,

such as birth, puberty, marriage, and death. Weddings and funerals, along with baby showers, are rites of passage in the American society. One of these rites centers around initiation. Initiation may have consisted of a buffalo hunt for a native American teenage boy a century ago. It could be the cutting off of a shirttail of a pilot who has just soloed.

Tongues function as an initiation rite for those neo-Pentecostal groups who insist on tongues as a sign of being baptized in the Spirit.

One cannot enter into such groups with full acceptance until he has experienced tongues. He may be welcomed at meetings, but group pressure will be subtly or openly present until he experiences tongues. When he does, there is great celebration. Tongues are therefore a token of group acceptance and at the same time a sign of godly power.

Thus, the rite of initiation, common in all societies, is for some neo-Pentecostals the demonstration of tongues.

Speaking in tongues is often discussed flippantly as if this gift were simple and came only to those who do not think about it. Those who do reflect on this phenomenon will know it immediately to be as complex as it is mysterious. Those who would understand the workings of God know the value of being open to the Spirit with an informed intellect. Those who speak of tongues indiscriminately, whether non-Pentecostal or neo-Pentecostal, do an injustice to those who would understand the workings of the Creator.

Conclusion

Those who do not speak in tongues should realize that tongues can be analyzed from many perspectives. So may the neo-Pentecostal Christians who seem so excited about their newfound power in the Spirit. To speak only from a biblical or psychological base is to miss part of the majesty of the new charismatics. They are deserving of a hearing from an informed base. Remarks like "Oh, he'll get over it" or "I know what that bunch is like" do not even begin to move toward understanding or openness.

For the new Pentecostal, the realization will come that the experience of tongues is much more profound than it seems at first. It may affect all of one's personality and deserve all the serious study it can get. To be baptized of the Spirit is to be honored with the challenge that God has reached down in mercy to assign the recipient with an important set of tasks. Tongues are an initiation, but the grace with which they are given can be stillborn if the brain dies on initial contact. The group into which one is initiated is only the beginning. A second step is reflection. The third step is toward the neighbor.

NOTES

1. Don Basham, *A Handbook on Holy Spirit Baptism* (Monroeville: Whitaker Books, 1971), p. 61.

2. Ibid., p. 65.

3. Quoted by Basham, pp. 70 ff.

4. Oral Roberts, *The Baptism with the Holy Spirit and the Value of Speaking in Tongues Today* (Tulsa: Oral Roberts Press, 1964), pp. 54 ff.

5. From *The Emory Magazine* (February 1974), p. 3.

6. Frank Stagg, *Glossolalia* (Nashville: Abingdon Press, 1967), p. 22.

7. Joseph Smith, "Articles of Faith," *History of the Church* 4 (Salt Lake City: Deseret Book Company), p. 541.

8. L. Carlyle May, "A Survey of Glossolalia and Related Phenomena in

Non-Christian Religions," *American Anthropologist* 58 (May 1956), pp. 75–96.

9. Quoted by V. Raymond Edman, "Divine or Devilish?" *Christian Herald* (May 1964), p. 16.

10. Morton T. Kelsey, *Tongue Speaking* (New York: Doubleday and Company, 1964), p. 194.

11. Erik Erikson, *Childhood and Society* (New York: W. W. Norton and Company, 1963), pp. 247 ff.

4. What to Do?

There they are, the new Pentecostals, in living black and white, and impossible to ignore when it comes to answering certain questions like:

1. What should our church do when suddenly some neo-Pentecostals appear in our midst?

2. How open should I be to the Spirit when complete openness could be divisive to our church?

3. What is there to be learned from the neo-Pentecostals?

4. Are tongues for the modern church?

5. What qualities of the Christian life are for every believer?

These qualities are found in Galatians 5:22–23 and are nine in number, although they are not to be viewed as separate. The fruit of the Spirit hang as one giant cluster together. It is no accident that Paul listed nine fruit (not fruits) in his letter to the Galatians. It is also no accident that there are nine grace gifts listed by Paul in 1 Corinthians 12. In the Christian life, this fruit of the Spirit operates in tandem with the gifts of the Spirit.

This tandem relationship is examined at the beginning of this chapter because it sets the tone for whatever happens that is wholesome when neo-Pentecostals meet non-Pentecostals. The fruit of the Spirit stands as a balance on the side of the seesaw opposite to gifts, with the Spirit in the middle. Gifts without the fruit are irrelevant and potentially divisive. The fruit without the gifts is sweet, but lacks complete empowering. It is only as they are seen in relationship that the gifts and the fruit are seen in their intended meaning for the believer. The non-Pentecostal who judges by the fruit only and the new Pentecostal who judges by gifts only are both out of balance on God's scales. This can be seen in the following chart:

Gifts	**Fruit**
Wisdom	*Love*
Knowledge	*Joy*
Faith	*Peace*
Healings	*Patience*
Exorcisms	*Gentleness*
Discernment	*Faith*
Tongues	*Meekness*
Interpretation	*Self-control*

Note the various ways in which this chart may be used in parallel. Wisdom appears at the head of the gifts list and love at the head of the fruit list. It is obvious that each is to be used in relationship with the other. Wisdom without love becomes dry speculation or uncaring, intellectual snobbery. Love without wisdom can result in foolish, sanguine waste.

One example I have seen of love without wisdom happened when there was a group of well-meaning women from the mother church that was sponsoring our mission. They came into a poverty-ridden community and gave out twenty-dollar bills indiscriminately to mothers. That night the neighborhood was turned into a drunken brawl. It took two days to get order restored and some hungry children fed who had been neglected while their mothers drank up twenty dollars worth of liquor.

Non-Pentecostals who feign a kind of wisdom toward their brothers and sisters in Christ who are charismatic, yet remain unloving, are doing about half of what God requires. New Pentecostals who claim to be loving while spreading tongues indiscriminately are also doing about half.

Interesting also is the pairing of healing with patience. A typical progression in Pentecostal circles is to move from tongues to healing. There is *no* doubt that God uses faith healing, faith healers, or faith in healing. It is also tragic when patience is not paired with promises of healings. It remains a mystery as to why some are healed and others are not. Patience is a balancing fruit to those who would promise healing automatically.

Particularly current is the pairing of exorcisms with gentleness. The traditional style of exorcism as pictured in "The Exorcist: Part 2" is anything but gentle, either for the priest or the client. There is a quiet confidence within the person who has the dual power of the Spirit and the Son. He can, therefore, be very gentle to the client who sees himself as filled with demons. This subject is particularly appropriate to that minority of new Pentecostals for whom the gifts of the Spirit have progressed from tongues to healing to exorcism.

There is little gentleness about the typical pattern of exorcism performed by those neo-Pentecostals who do exorcisms, sometimes called a "deliverance ministry." This ministry frequently deals with demons one at a time and subjects the client to long hours of physical, emotional, and spiritual duress. The client is often asked to come back the following evening when other demons will be encountered.

How many demons are there in the world today? Probably not as many as some new Pentecostals think and more than most evangelicals think.[1] There is a strong power in the way Jesus cast out demons all at once. There is a correlation between gentleness resting in Christ's power and casting out demons in the power of the Spirit.

Note the correlation between preaching and goodness. The word translated *goodness* means totality or wholeness. The function of preaching is, at least partly, to bring healing wholeness to the hearers. Any preaching in the Spirit will bring healing to those upset by others' being divisive while claiming to be of the Spirit.

Perhaps the most significant matchup for discussion of the new Pentecostal movement is the one between tongues and meekness. The word *meekness* usually brings mental pictures of being passive, quiet, and a bit sissy. (Though it is not literally accurate to read "meekness" here, there is something good to be said for this traditional rendering. Those who speak in tongues should be quiet doing so, especially at first, until spiritual maturity catches up with spiritual ecstasy.)

The Greek word usually read meekness should be translated *discipline* and was the same one used to describe a fine team of horses such as those that pulled Roman chariots in the days of Paul. The tongues-speaker should exhibit discipline lest he become ineffective in other parts of his continuing Christian growth. But the other imbalance is just as weak. Discipline without ecstasy in the

WHAT TO DO?

Christian walk is stale asceticism.

Besides reading the chart horizontally to discover enlightening matchups in Christian balance, it is also important to note which qualities are listed first and which last.

On the gift list, wisdom comes first. If there is any one quality which their non-Pentecostal brothers often pray for for their neo-Pentecostal friends, it is good judgment (wisdom). The grace gifts are to be used in equal parts of enthusiasm and wisdom.

Listed last are tongues and their interpretation. They are not listed last for emphasis. It is clear throughout 1 Corinthians 12—15 that, for Paul at least, tongues were the least important of the gifts of grace.

Note also that love heads the list of the fruit of the Spirit. Just as in 1 Corinthians 13, Paul wanted to emphasize that the greatest quality for Christians on both sides of the Pentecost issue is patient love.

There are other parallels to be drawn from these two lists on the chart. Note that knowledge brings joy. Normally Christians do not think of knowledge and joy together. Ask any Christian who has just lost a Christian parent in death. He will tell you that the knowledge of God's care for his own beyond death brings a quiet joy that enables the believer to see through the tears. Note also that joy is balanced with knowledge.

There is much more to be drawn from these parallels, but on to more practical matters.

Hey, wait just a minute! Mr. Author, you promised me, the reader, some practical advice in this chapter. Here you started with a lot of Bible study. What's practical about that?

Mr. Reader, this is your author speaking. There is

nothing more practical than the base of the Spirit to deal with things of the Spirit. Until all of God's children display the fruit, God's children will continue to quarrel like the infants we are without the Spirit.

There are some alternatives to the quarreling that continues needlessly between the Spirit-baptized and the Spirit-filled. These are practical suggestions for bringing peace with love and joy. The fruit is part of a holy cluster.

There are some church situations in which the fruit is held in high esteem and used by the members. In these churches, the Lord reigns supreme. These churches have mixed the Spirit with some practical steps.

Oral Roberts makes some strong suggestions for those who speak in tongues. He says:

1. You are responsible for the use of this gift.

2. You are responsible for understanding the function of your gift and for knowing how and when to exercise it.

3. You are responsible for being in control of your spirit.

Mr. Roberts closes his train of thought by reminding his readers, "The Lord may not manifest a gift in us because of our worthiness, but we have to be worthy in our character to exercise it effectively." [2]

Oral Roberts' emphasis on responsibility sets the tone for the remainder of this chapter. The responsible Christian on both sides of the Spirit issue will exercise his responsibility in love by keeping in mind certain guidelines.

For the non-Pentecostals, on the non-Pentecostal side, it is important that Pentecostals and tongues-speakers not be equated in even initial impression. Many in the neo-Pentecostal ranks do not speak in tongues and choose not

WHAT TO DO?

to as a matter of principle. Perhaps their reason is that they have seen their charismatic friends abuse the gift; perhaps they have once spoken in tongues but now see that gift as one of the least important; perhaps these nontongues-speakers simply exercise other gifts, such as prophecy, which they deem more important. Whatever the reason, there are many who do not speak in tongues, but still stand central to the neo-Pentecostal movement.

Further, the non-Pentecostal Christian should be open to the leadership of the Spirit in his life. One certain result is being filled with the Spirit, along with a resultant presence of the Spirit that leads to a sensitivity to the "least of these" who are Christ in the world.

Third, the non-Pentecostal should operate on the basis that tongues are legitimate twentieth-century gifts of the Spirit.

Those who are currently contesting the validity of tongues as a modern gift of the Spirit, especially in relation to the neo-Pentecostal movement, usually do so from one of two perspectives. It is either argued that the tongues are inherently demonic or that tongues, along with miracles, were ended after the first century. The second argument usually proceeds along the line that these signs and miracles were needed as a validation for the early apostles.

Those who argue that tongues are demonic must confront the fact that Paul called tongues a gift of the Spirit and indeed participated in tongues-speaking himself. Paul's remarks against tongues were entirely about their abuse in the body of Christ. Would Paul have practiced and called a phenomenon a gift of the Spirit unless it was? The neat and quick labeling of tongues as demonic raises a serious question as to biblical authenticity.

Regarding the second argument, the New Testament nowhere teaches that the spiritual gifts were given solely to authenticate the apostles or that they, along with miracles, were to cease after the first century or apostolic age. More specifically, Paul did not teach the cessation of tongues or other spiritual gifts at the close of the first century. It is true that he made reference in 1 Corinthians 13:10 to the time when "that which is perfect is come." Given the context of Paul's argument (especially chap. 15, in which Paul spoke specifically about the resurrection of Christ), he must have been referring to the second coming of Christ. So Paul was saying that the gifts are to be measured by love and are to cease at the Lord's return—not before.

Fourth, the non-Pentecostal should welcome the new Pentecostal into full Christian fellowship at the local church level. Divisions over such matters as tongues are as much the fault of the nontongues Christians as any other. Those who criticize the tongues practitioner for making that gift the test of fellowship for admission into a charismatic group should go very slowly in calling tongues the one sign that disallows open and friendly fellowship. Tongues are not a decisive factor in determining whether one is a Christian and ready for fellowship among a body of confessed sinful believers.

Churches need not split when tongues break out among the believers. Paul left room within the worship format of a body of believers for such manifestations if practiced with restraint and love. Paul did place four restrictions on the use of such worthy enterprises as evangelism. Some of the persons God is using most profitably in evangelistic

WHAT TO DO? 73

enterprises today are among the neo-Pentecostals. They ask simply for the courtesy of being heard, even in an unknown tongue on occasion.

Fifth, the non-Pentecostal should praise God for the new power that God is infusing into the lives of his followers through the outpouring of his Spirit in these days. If the common abuses accompany this outpouring, constantly pray for patient love to overlook these abuses, even when circumstances are difficult.

Sixth, the non-Pentecostal should not be disturbed by the fact that one of the more visible gifts has not been given to him. This does not inherently mean that he is a second-class citizen in God's kingdom or (as is hinted by some overzealous neo-Pentecostals) not a Christian at all. An immature Christian will be easily threatened by such occurrences as an occasional visit by a Jehovah's Witness who is able to quote more verses as prooftexts than he.

He will also likely be made to feel insecure or even paranoid by one who insists that he is not a Christian unless he speaks in tongues or attends a rally or goes visiting for the church. The fact that the more visible gifts are not apparent in a specific Christian's case does not make that Christian inferior. He may be able to practice 1 Corinthians 13 while others debate chapters 12 and 14. When the Spirit is present, he gives assurance to those momentarily threatened or angry.

Seventh, the non-Pentecostal son of God should not be closed to the Spirit. It may be that other gifts are more important for the building up of the body of Christ. It is ideal for the Christian not to repudiate or deny anything that the Spirit has already done in any believer's life, is doing at the present, or desires to do in the future. The open Christian is simply opening the way for the Spirit to do more.

Finally, the non-Pentecostal should be open to the entire work of the Holy Spirit. He does energizing work outside the list of gifts listed in 1 Corinthians 12. Those who are being constantly filled with the Spirit already have evidences that God's continuing presence does some beautiful things for the believer. He cleanses from sin—and specific sins—and allows the disciple to accept forgiveness even when this is most difficult. The feeling of standing before the light of God as cleaned through confession is one that many know only through the Spirit.

The Spirit also empowers for witness. More than one stammering tongue since Moses has been made to speak truth when the Spirit controls. Weak believers have seen the beauty of new Christians because they know that the Spirit gives utterance even in the presence of unbelievers. The Spirit also relaxes those who are most nervous about being a disciple. Those forced into uncomfortable situations have been made boldly confident by the Spirit.

Further, the Spirit is sent to lead the seeker to all truth. This does not mean that the brain is by-passed, but that the Spirit gives impetus to the process of giving wisdom and knowledge to those who seek them. Those engaged in daily social ministry to other human beings know one of the fillings of the Spirit. That is the constancy that the Spirit gives. Even when there is no visible response on the part of the client, the minister can keep on helping (hopefully with wisdom) when the Spirit gives "stickability."

To be closed to the Spirit because one does not like the way in which the Spirit is manifesting himself to another disciple is to run two risks. First, it is not good to judge another believer. Only God can do that. Backslidden Baptists and Methodists behave similarly. Perhaps only God can or should judge them. The second risk the non-Pentecostal may run by judging the neo-Pentecostal quickly is the risk of grieving the Spirit. The numerous advantages of being filled with the Spirit, to both the believer and those with whom he ministers, may be cut off or slowed down if one is closed to the Spirit and those baptized by the Spirit.

Oral Roberts is right! The key word is *responsibility*. The responsible non-Pentecostal will avoid overreaction to what may prove to be the whim of the moment instead of a legitimate leading of the Spirit.

For the Neo-Pentecostal

Those who are a part of the new charismatics must realize that they have a responsibility to those among the believers who are not yet so intensely turned on by the Spirit. If, indeed, the neo-Pentecostal has a message to convey to the rest of Christendom, he can do it best by following a few scriptural and/or practical guidelines. These include:

1. Admit that some neo-Pentecostals are abusing the gifts of the Spirit. Some non-Pentecostals cannot see the Spirit for the abuses. Admission that there are some abuses frees both parties for a fruit (of the Spirit)–ful conversation—maybe even for fellowship.

2. The neo-Pentecostal should not expect all of his Christian brothers to exercise the same gift, whether it be tongues or wisdom. This is to deny that brother the right to express the same experience of baptism by the Spirit through another Christian symbol. The expectation that

all will have one gift has led to much of the misunderstanding among the children of God.

3. The neo-Pentecostal should not take an attitude of superiority to those who do not participate in the movement. This feeling can be conveyed very subtly, especially by those who once had a type of discipleship that was lifeless. That discipleship was given life by the Spirit in due form does not mean that all are lifeless without a similar experience. The feeling that lifeless is synonymous with non-Pentecostal is sometimes conveyed by neo-Pentecostals. This attitude does not lend itself to wholesome sharing. The Spirit gives patience and meekness.

4. The neo-Pentecostal should realize that the baptism of the Spirit does not make one a theological expert or biblical scholar immediately. Rash statements based on a few selected passages from Acts or Romans or Ephesians do not a Bible scholar make. Careful study in the newfound freshness of the Spirit over a period of months (at least) will be necessary before one can speak with any authority about such matters as how and when spiritual gifts are to be practiced.

Remember that no one has a corner on spiritual knowledge, that we are all weak vessels and must walk humbly before God and his family. In the flush of a new spiritual experience, neo-Pentecostals are sometimes swept off their feet. Their judgment becomes temporarily unreliable. Time will tell whether the experience be of the Spirit.

5. The neo-Pentecostal should exercise that fruit of the Spirit called patience. It will be helpful to remember what the previous attitude was toward all Pentecostals. Many in Christendom are ill equipped, because of Pentecostal

WHAT TO DO?

abuses or inbred biases, to hear what newly Spirit-baptized Christians have to say. Patience will be necessary if the message of the Spirit's power is to be heard.

6. The neo-Pentecostal should appreciate his own historic church setting. There have been centuries of traditions in such matters as forms of public worship. These forms, as in need of reform as most are, are not likely to be dropped immediately. On a local church level, the destruction of an entire church's fellowship "for the sake of the Spirit" is a contradiction within itself. There are many in the churches who need a refreshing of the Spirit. They may never experience it if the neo-Pentecostal is seen as a troublemaker.

7. The neo-Pentecostal should avoid the easy way at first of pulling away from the church and going only where he is likely to be understood and his gifts recognized. A sympathetic hearing should not be a priority, at least in the sense of seeking it only.

8. The neo-Pentecostal should look again to the same Spirit who baptized him in the first place. That same Spirit of God brings the fruit with the gifts. Pray for patience and peace to give the victory over bitterness that may result from not being appreciated or even given a hearing at first.

9. If tongues are involved, they should be used primarily in private devotions. This new dimension of private prayer may open up new avenues of Christian ministry, but not if thwarted early by means of public ridicule by those less understanding.

10. Be quiet and peaceful about your own experience. Arguments about baptism of the Spirit are of little help unless that baptism is accompanied by the life of the fruit

of his Spirit. Make sure that the new testimony of your words is matched by the testimony of your life.

In summary, the reaction of the neo-Pentecostal to being filled with the Spirit should be to move slowly, sharing new experiences with those who will listen. This is not a very glamorous route, but the fellowship of a church may be preserved. The ministry of a changed life will be effective in the long run.

For the Whole Church

When neo-Pentecostals become evident within what has been historically a non-Pentecostal church, there are some immediate steps to be taken both by church leadership and the entire body. These include:

1. *Bible study.*—The Holy Spirit did not suddenly burst into existence when several neo-Pentecostals made their baptism in the Spirit known publicly within your congregational fellowship. Bible perspectives on the Spirit concerning incidents and issues will be necessary to deal with the outpouring of that same Spirit. (See chap. 2 of this book for helps.)

The pastor may want to schedule a series of sermons or Wednesday-evening Bible lessons on what the Word says about the Spirit. The time to begin is now. Waiting until the crisis created by an overzealous neo-Pentecostal is upon a congregation is ill advised. The Bible in its total teaching on the Spirit can give a peace over instantaneous mayhem.

2. *Keep the alarm level low.*—Panic has set into many a congregation when a well-meaning disciple burst into tongues during a Sunday evening service. This occurrence should be no more disturbing or alarming than another

disciple's asking to give a testimony (particularly if an interpreter is present). Overreaction at this point can divide the congregation as to what they think happened and why.

About 1970 one Baptist pastor in Kansas had the tongues phenomenon hit his church suddenly. He used what he called the *"Well"* technique of counseling. Those engaged in a Monday-night prayer service came to the pastor and said, "You must meet with us Monday night. What we've got, you need." He replied, *"Well,* not this time." Those in the congregation not in the Monday night meetings came to the pastor and said, "We have to call a meeting this Wednesday night to vote these people out of the church before they tear it up." The pastor replied, *"Well,* not this week."

In the meantime, he preached a series of six sermons on the Spirit. A period of ninety days passed. Those speaking in tongues soon saw they were not going to receive undue attention. Those non-Pentecostals in the church were allowed neither to take complete control nor to be considered second-class members for not having the gifts. Those who were of the Spirit started displaying the fruit. The fellowship was preserved. Renewal came, partly because the alarm level was kept low.

3. *Hold an open forum early.*—A pastor in Oklahoma came to a session in which I lectured on neo-Pentecostals. He went home angry and wrote me a letter of protest because I had not castigated those troublemaking neo-Pentecostals who were trying to take over his church by talking to members without ever confronting him. I wrote back, suggesting that he preach on John 15 on Sunday morning and hold an open forum on the Spirit that same

evening. The largest Sunday evening crowd in the history of the church, of course, gathered for the forum. Both sides were allowed to speak.

The meeting lasted two hours. A spirit of renewal swept the congregation, and no church split resulted. Very few instances of trouble arose again, perhaps partly due to the open forum. This approach keeps both sides from operating on the basis of rumors.

4. *Take a long look.*—Sociologically, it took forty years or more for the great religious movements of the last century to come and go. The second Great Awakening is just such an instance. Today, with a great communications network and the American society's tendency to join anything new in the religious scene, from Transcendental Meditation to the Unification Church, a movement can come and go in less than a decade. The Jesus freaks of 1970 are now relics of the past.

Groups and individuals within the neo-Pentecostal movement also tend to run a cycle. This cycle is frequently baptism of the Spirit and is sometimes accompanied by tongues and an emphasis on healing and exorcism. The cycle can run its course in a few months or years.

Those churches that have overreacted by negative censure of those involved in the neo-Pentecostal movement have cut these participants off prematurely from what is needed most—the fellowship of the church. When the neo-Pentecostal movement has run its course, those involved will be very slow to drift back toward the churches that censured them.

The long look will prevent hasty judgment of a movement bound to take new forms.

Those evangelicals who complained loudest about the

WHAT TO DO?

social-action emphasis in church in the late 1960s are those who complain loudest now that the emphasis is on the movement of the Spirit. The pendulum swings. The disciple who can survive change is the one who can remain genuinely concerned, patient, and knowledgeable of the cycles of history without being lulled to sleep by the swing of the pendulum.

5. *Avoid the formation of cliques in the church.*—The haves and have-nots within churches having a neo-Pentecostal element tend to drift apart. There are those who meet in the small-group fellowship meetings and those who do not. If the groups are to meet, they should not be exclusive or half-secret. These groups should meet either in the church building or in the home of a respected leader in the church. No one should be forced to come to this kind of group, but no one should be excluded. Everyone should be welcomed.

6. *Encourage individual decisions.*—Each person within the congregation should be encouraged to come to his own decision about the various gifts of the Spirit. None of the gifts are for every Christian, as is the case with every fruit. The question is not "What should the *congregation* do about the grace gifts?" but whether the Spirit leads persons to have certain gifts governed by the *agape* love of 1 Corinthians 13.

A congregation that allows such freedom will never be accused of forcing the Spirit underground. Further, it will not give fuel to the fire of those who feel compelled to gain attention by being different. Because the Spirit blows where he will, each Christian will be unique.

Conclusion

The pouring out of the Holy Spirit in these days is spontaneous. Attempting to program him by proclaiming or voting that he cannot flow through a certain church or area is as futile as trying to catch a whirlwind with a net. Yet, there are those who try continually to confine the Spirit to one gift or congregation or movement. John 3:8, "The wind bloweth where it listeth," is very important for understanding the present movement of the Spirit.

Winds of change are blowing. They may blow next into your local situation—indeed, into your soul. When they come, may they be received with responsibility and openness—to the winds, to the persons affected, and to your own heart's reaction.

The winds of change that be of the Spirit are healing winds—especially if they are accepted in the spirit of patience. The result may be churches awakened. The prayer of Jesus that all his disciples be one can be a reality. Winds of the Spirit do not bring chaos, but anxious disciples can. May God grant each of us the gentle goodness which the Spirit brings—sometimes even in a whirlwind.

NOTES

1. See M. Thomas Starkes, *The Occult as Option* (Orlando: Christ for the World, Inc., 1973), for more information on demons and exorcism.

2. Oral Roberts, *The Baptism with the Holy Spirit and the Value of Speaking in Tongues Today* (Tulsa: Oral Roberts Press, 1964), pp. 54 ff.

Conclusion: The Late 1970s Amid Winds

Here they come, ready or not! They are the new Pentecostals, who are likely to be different from the old Pentecostals the rest of Christendom have been used to dealing with. They are different in that they:

• Almost unanimously choose to remain within their own fellowship rather than starting denominations of their own.

• Are mildly charismatic in that typical abuses are missing in such matters as displaying the gifts. Pandemonium is replaced by a limited amount of liturgical order.

• Display little interest in the old idea of perfectionism. They are as likely to have short or long hair, wear makeup and jewelry, and go dancing as any mainline Presbyterian.

• Have little or no ties to some suprastructure with an international headquarters. National magazines and structure are the exception.

• Exhibit openly their newfound joy. There is little of the serious, long-faced piety some still associate with organized Pentecostalism.

• Have meetings that are informal, geared to meeting personal needs by "getting inside" those present. Larger rallies are rare.

• Come from a wide range of educational, social, economic, and denominational settings. A Catholic plumber is likely to "sing in the Spirit" next to an Episcopalian lawyer. These ecumenical strands are leading to a truly integrated church of the Spirit.

- Usually do not require tongues as a sign of being genuinely Christian.

Here they come, blown along by the winds of the Spirit. To confront them as if they were the old Pentecostals is to misunderstand them, almost completely.

Upon reflection and understanding, the neo-Pentecostals are still getting mixed reviews. Most agree that the excitement and joy of the Spirit's presence are needed in traditional churches and that the neo-Pentecostals may supply that much-needed vigor.

Kenneth L. Pogard of California, serving as coordinator of the American Baptist Charismatic Fellowship, says, "God is doing a great thing today. This movement is going to have a real impact in renewing the churches." [1]

Whatever the source, new Pentecostal or non-Pentecostal, the agreement comes on the point that there is now a renewed appreciation of the Spirit. He is seen now in his glory as the motivating and enabling force that makes the Christian experience more than dry dogma and boring ritual. This has prompted some formerly scornful Christians to suspect that they just might have something to learn from neo-Pentecostals.

The fact that neo-Pentecostalism is attracting followers by the hundreds of thousands cannot be ignored by the more traditional churches. This is especially true when the bulk of neo-Pentecostals are coming from within (and staying there with the gift of the Spirit) these traditional churches. The recurring refrain from the letters to the seven churches of Asia in the Revelation seems relevant:

CONCLUSION: THE LATE 1970s AMID WINDS

"Let him that has ears to hear listen to what the Spirit is saying to the churches."

At the very least, even a grudging outsider can concede to the new Pentecostals that they offer something that many persons are seeking—a direct, personal experience of the reality of God. This direct experience is contagious, as is the conversion experience that has been the lifeline of the evangelical form of Christianity. The commonality of experience can add to the level of acceptance between evangelicals and new Pentecostals, if both groups are willing to enter into dialogue.

At the same time, more traditional evangelicals can offer to the neo-Pentecostals the gentle reminder that experience alone is not a legitimate criterion for determining true spirituality. Religious experience comes in many forms, ranging from a Billy Graham crusade to the Moslem who beats himself annually on the back with a whip until the blood flows. This flow of blood is supposedly done to win the grace of Allah. Experience must be balanced by wisdom. This wisdom is precisely what the evangelical offers the neo-Pentecostal.

Rules for dialogue among Christians, therefore, are worthy of consideration here. Both sides will find these guidelines helpful:

1. *Do not compare the strengths of one movement with the weaknesses of the other.* This practice can be done *ad infinitum*, but adds nothing to the fair task of mutual understanding. The Spirit will have little to do with pseudo dialogue that is not reflective of his fruit.

2. *Avoid sharp personal attack.* Personality assassination with such statements as "Oh, we know that church and its people. It's as cold as a clam" has no more place in

Christian understanding than "All those Pentecostals are neurotics who can't cut it anywhere else."

3. *Listen until understanding comes.* True dialogue has occurred only when one party can repeat the premises of the other to the satisfaction of that Christian partner in dialogue. Each may retain the right to disagree, but understanding has occurred only when feedback indicates an intense listening. Dialogue has not occurred when one talks while the other waits until he can get the floor and prove his next point.

4. *Examine the biblical witness together.* For each to continue quoting his dozen or so favorite verses without being challenged by new evidence leads to a type of deadness which cannot be of the Spirit. The Spirit leads to truth through the written Word and the living Word (Jesus). That is his function. True dialogue helps this experience happen.

The neo-Pentecostal movement can bring its vitality to the churches and the non-Pentecostal churches can lend their theological strength to the movement only when the dialogue described above continues.

Where can it happen?

- on street corners or wherever informed Christians meet
- in retreat settings
- in clergy conferences
- in youth Bible studies
- in home fellowship Bible discussions
- in Sunday-evening joint worship services
- in Thursday-evening prayer groups
- elsewhere—as long as *responsibility* and *responsibility* (the ability and willingness to respond to each

CONCLUSION: THE LATE 1970s AMID WINDS

other and to the Spirit) are present.

In dialogue, the basic human needs of community, intimacy, and acceptance can be realized. These deeply felt needs are part of what started the neo-Pentecostal movement in the first place.

This new element of community can keep the work of daily ministry to the secular world from going stale. Christian vitality is found in response to the full spectrum of human need. This call to the world goes on in spite of passing winds and can be revitalized through contact with those who are baptized with the Spirit. The story of *The Cross and the Switchblade* is evidence that the Holy Spirit does lend his power to the work of caring for God's children. Those concerned with social ministries and social action can certainly stand an occasional spiritual shot in the heart, which comes from being touched anew by the Spirit.

The Christian task of constant human concern can be revitalized when one realizes that right action springs from loving one another. This love runs less risk of becoming a dead law when it is touched again and again by the enabling power of the Spirit. Perhaps that is why Jesus promised his disciples the presence of the Spirit as a sign of his continual presence with them in the world.

The Spirit's renewing power is not confined to the spectrum of social concern. His work is much broader than that. The charismatic renewal speaks to the dilemma of many Christians who oscillate between a lukewarm haze and a religious fogbank. To the proud, the Spirit brings humility. To the depressed, the Spirit gives comfort. To the mourning, he presents joy.

There is one catch, however. It may be called "Catch

13:7" (1 Cor.). There Paul said that love believes, hopes, and endures "all things." This openness of which Paul spoke can lead to freedom in the Spirit, and not all persons (even those in Christ) are ready to be set completely free from sins or anger or their "half-saved" state. Most persons who are forced to choose between freedom and security will choose security. Within the church that security may be found in ritual, dogma, or worship. The Spirit's effort to set believers free often goes unclaimed. The neo-Pentecostal movement only accents that fact. But the winds blow on.

When the winds blow to the individual believer, they call for balance in at least three categories:

1. *The total disciple.*—Jesus, when asked to name the great commandment, restated the Deuteronomic injunction that God is to be loved with all one's "heart, soul, mind, and strength."

The presence of neo-Pentecostals on the religious scene makes this call for total-personality discipleship. Those led by the Spirit too often exhibit a tendency to be anti-intellectual. Oral Roberts states, for example, that in order to be ready to receive "the gift of the Holy Ghost," one must "be willing to bypass the intellect." [2] This attitude has led the intellectual community to remain somewhat skeptical about the neo-Pentecostal movement. Such statements indicate a partial understanding of discipleship.

The personality aspects of the disciple are to be held in balance. The Spirit-filled person is filled throughout his personality. The non-Pentecostal who remains so intellectual that he knows not the fullness of the Spirit is only a partial disciple, as well.

CONCLUSION: THE LATE 1970s AMID WINDS 89

When the Spirit comes, he does not turn the believer into a sponge, a vegetable, or a robot. The total personality is enlivened and enriched, not emasculated, fragmented, or eradicated. One could wonder about genuineness of experience when he hears a minority of neo-Pentecostals say such things as "Since I got the Spirit, I don't have to make any more decisions. He just handles everything" or "I had to give up my volunteer work at the hospital. I've been so busy going to the meetings."

Quietly, step by step, the Spirit claims and enlivens every aspect of the believer's personality when he comes in fullness. He does not highlight any part of the personality in distinction to or in injury of any other part.

2. *The cross-shaped ethic.*—In defining Christian discipleship, Martin Luther said it should be cross-shaped. Jesus said much the same thing when he said that the disciple is to love both God and neighbor. The vertical relationship is the one between the believer and God. The Spirit comes often to give vitality to that relationship. Praise, joy, celebration, and spiritual maturity are all aspects of that relationship.

The horizontal relationship (the one with the disciple's neighbor) does not stop with being filled with the Spirit. The Spirit more properly enables the disciple to minister more completely with the needy neighbor.

A balance between the horizontal and vertical is required for complete discipleship. Anyone who claims the power of the Spirit and does not immediately begin a fuller ministry to the needs of his neighbors had better reexamine that claim.

As an Alabama Baptist leader said, "The first time the new Pentecostals put up a clothing box on the corner like the Salvation Army, I will be forced to take the movement more seriously." This horizontal-vertical balance can eliminate those Christians who are either "so heavenly they're no earthly good" or "so earthly they're no heavenly good."

3. *The persons within the Trinity.*—The importance of *each* of the persons in the Trinity cannot be exaggerated for the growing disciple. Many attempts have been made to fragment the Trinity. One way of splitting it is to say that the Father ruled during the Old Testament era, the Son during his lifetime, and the Spirit ever since.

Such fragmentation overlooks the fact that where the Son is, there are the Father and the Spirit. Those involved in any controversy over the neo-Pentecostal movement should remember that where the Spirit is, there are also the Son and the Father. To be baptized by the Spirit and then cease to mention the name of Jesus is to neglect the balance that is a natural part of the Trinity.

On the other hand, to be so jealous of the role of Jesus that one is closed to the work of the Spirit is to miss part of the point as well. Unitarianism is easy to understand when it is practiced by Unitarians. That group worships only the Father as God. It is more difficult to understand when one of the other two persons of the Trinity is worshiped to the neglect of the other two. Although harder to comprehend, it is no less dangerous to the unity of God in relation to the believers.

To maintain these balances is to respond in integrity to the challenges and calls of the neo-Pentecostal movement. Any partial response to that challenge is just that.

True discipleship is anchored in the historical Jesus, given visible human expression by active love, and thematically true to the Bible. Inauthentic discipleship is given visible expression by egocentric works, does not particularly glorify Jesus, and chooses only a few isolated verses as the guide for growth. Attempts to manipulate, squelch, program, or artificially induce the Spirit are evidences of inauthentic discipleship. The Spirit goes where he wills. Let all Christians hear the blowing of his presence and respond in loving acceptance and responsibility.

All Christians are described in Hebrews as "partakers of the Holy Spirit who have tasted the powers of the age to come." The partaking varies in quantity, but the quality of the Spirit is uniform. This uniformity of spirit can characterize both the non-Pentecostal and the new Pentecostal. That unity within the body will come when the non-Pentecostals dare to be "irreverent" and the new Pentecostals lose their tendency to be "irrelevant."

The winds of change blow on. Let him who has the courage to experience—EXPERIENCE.

Notes

1. Quoted by George W. Cornell, "New Movement Gains in Churches," *The Atlanta Journal* (28 May 1971), p. 25A.

2. Oral Roberts, *The Baptism with the Holy Spirit and the Value of Speaking in Tongues Today* (Tulsa: Oral Roberts Press, 1964), p. 42.

Bibliography

I. MATERIALS FROM NEW PENTECOSTAL SOURCES

Several publishing houses and centers for information deal exclusively with new Pentecostal materials, including books, tapes, filmstrips, and tracts.

Logos International
185 North Avenue
Plainfield, N.J. 07060

Christian Growth Ministries
Box 306
Ft. Lauderdale, FL. 32203

Whitaker Books
504 Laurel Drive
Monroeville, PA. 15146

Ave Maria Press
Notre Dame
Notre Dame, IN. 46556

Watchung Book Service
P. O. Box 292
Watchung, N.J. 07061

Society for Pentecostal Studies
Box 122
Franklin Springs, GA. 30639

The *Logos Journal* may be obtained by subscription from Logos International.

New Covenant is available by subscription from Box 102, Main St. Station, Ann Arbor, MI. 48107.

II. CURRENT CRITICAL INTERPRETATIONS

Durasoff, Steve. *Bright Wind of the Spirit: Pentecostalism Today*. Englewood Cliffs, New Jersey: Prentice-Hall, 1973.

Hollenweger, Walter J. *The Pentecostals: the Charismatic Movement in the Churches*. Minneapolis: Augsburg Publishing House, 1972.

Kildahl, John P. *The Psychology of Speaking in Tongues*. New York: Harper and Row, 1972.

Nichol, John Thomas. *Pentecostalism*. Plainfield, New Jersey: Logos Books, 1972.

O'Connor, Edward D. *The Pentecostal Movement in the Catholic Church*. Notre Dame: Ave Maria Press, 1971.

Samarin, William J. *Tongues of Men and Angels: The Religious Language of Pentecostalism*. New York: The Macmillan Company, 1972.

III. Sympathetic Books on the New Pentecostalism

Basham, Don. *Deliver Us from Evil*. Washington Depot, Connecticut: Chosen Books, 1972.

Boone, Pat. *A New Song*. Carol Stream, Illinois: Creation House, 1970.

Carothers, Merlin. *Power in Praise*. Plainfield, New Jersey: Logos International, 1972.

Gelpi, Donald L., S. J. *Pentecostal Piety*. New York, New York: Paulist Press, 1972.

Kuhlman, Kathryn. *God Can Do It Again*. Englewood Cliffs, New Jersey: Prentice-Hall, 1969.

Larson, Bruce. *Ask Me to Dance*. Waco, Texas: Word Books, 1972.

Roberts, Oral. *The Baptism with the Holy Spirit*. Tulsa, Oklahoma: Oral Roberts, 1964.

Saint, Phil. *Amazing Saints*. Plainfield, New Jersey: Logos International, 1972.

_____. *With the Holy Spirit and with Fire*. Waco, Texas: Word Books, 1972.

Saloff-Astakhoff, N. I. *The Holy Spirit, His Work and Pentecostalism.* Berne, Indiana: Publishers Printing House, 1967.

Starkey, Lycurgus M., Jr. *The Holy Spirit at Work in the Church.* Nashville, Tennessee: Abingdon Press, 1965.

───────. *The Jesus Walk.* Old Tappan, New Jersey: Fleming H. Revell, 1972.

IV. OFFICIAL DENOMINATIONAL STATEMENTS

Several of the large church bodies have published helpful studies of new Pentecostalism for general distribution. These include:

A Report on Glossolalia, 1962. The American Lutheran Church, 422 S. Fifth St., Minneapolis, MN. 55415.

Preliminary Report, Study Commission on Glossolalia, The Episcopal Church, Diocese of California, 1055 Taylor St., San Francisco, CA. 94108.